Sven D. Olensky

STAYING HUMAN
IN THE AGE OF
ARTIFICIAL INTELLIGENCE

Securing the Human Core
through AI Orchestration Literacy

Printed in the United States of America

Paperback ISBN 979-8-9994400-9-9
Hardcover ISBN 979-8-9994400-2-0
eBook ISBN 979-8-9994400-0-6

First Edition: July 2025

Cover design created by the author using AI-assisted
design tools.

Cover Image Prompt:
*A single visible but faint glowing human fingerprint.
It is surrounded by very visible abstract digital noise,
circuit patterns and a softly glowing neural network. Blue
background, subtle lighting, minimalist design.
Background is visible. Top-centered composition, clean
negative space for text. Futuristic but organic feel. High
contrast, sharp detail.*

Agency *(n.)*

The capacity to act with awareness, to make choices deliberately, and to take ownership of their consequences. Agency is what allows a person to live with intention rather than drift on autopilot. It is not about control over systems: it is about control over *oneself*.

At its core, agency is the willingness to be present: to observe one's own actions, to make decisions with conscience, and to accept accountability for what follows. It resists the urge to outsource judgment. It refuses the comfort of default settings. It insists that every action is authored, not just executed.

Agency is not automatic. It must be exercised, again and again, especially when ease, speed, or consensus invite disengagement. To act with agency is to take responsibility for your presence in the world - for what you shape, what you permit, and what you let pass.

In the context of this book, agency is the ground from which all meaningful engagement begins. Without it, nothing else holds. Not learning. Not action. Not change.

Orchestration Literacy *(n.)*

The ability to shape the behavior of generative systems with purpose and precision. It's not about using AI fluently - it's about using it responsibly. *Orchestration literacy* means knowing what you're asking, why you're asking it, and how to evaluate what comes back.

It's the skill of stepping in when output misfires. It means catching when tone shifts, when bias creeps in, or when the answer looks smooth but says nothing. It's knowing how to reframe, how to press further, or when to stop and think before accepting the result. It means to have *agency*.

This is not a technical specialty. It's a civic skill. Just as reading lets you navigate a world of text, orchestration literacy lets you navigate a world of generated language. Without it, you're stuck in passive mode - scanning, reacting, complying.

With it, you stay in the loop. You lead the exchange. You remain the author of your intent.

PREFACE

A few years ago, this entire project would have been *impossible*.

No publisher would have picked up a concept like orchestration literacy from someone without academic credentials or institutional backing. No nonprofit would be taken seriously without seed funding, an advisory board, or a polished communications team. No curriculum would reach civic leaders, parents, educators, and small business owners - unless filtered through a university, a think tank, or a tech company's PR strategy.

But here I am. One person, a set of tools and a vision.

I didn't wait for permission. I did not have to ask anyone.

I used AI: not to replace my work, but to amplify it. To allow me to make my dreams become reality.

This is what AI literacy means in the age of agency. This is the entire point.

It's about reclaiming strategic capacity in a world that's rapidly shifting and where the people who understand how to work <u>with</u> AI, not just <u>for</u> it, will become the architects of our civic future.

<u>I'm nobody special.</u> I just had a sense that something needed to be built. And the courage to try.

And now that it's real, I want you to see that it's possible for you, too.

This isn't about expertise. It's about purpose. It's about using the tools of the moment to orchestrate a world we can live in... with dignity, literacy, and agency intact.

And if this work resonates with you, then let's not waste time.
Let's teach it. Let's share it. Let's make it the foundation.

July 2025
Sven D. Olensky
Founder, AI Literacy for Everyone Foundation

Why I wrote this Book

I didn't write this book in a burst of inspiration. It came together slowly, through late-night frustration, difficult conversations, and a constant back-and-forth with a machine I was using to clarify my own thoughts. That tension is part of the point. I've spent my life questioning systems that expect compliance without justification. I never accepted authority just because it existed. It had to prove it deserved to be there. That instinct started young, shaped by growing up in postwar Germany and learning early what happens when people follow without thinking. I stood up to bullies. I asked hard questions. And I watched how education systems taught the opposite.

School was never designed to develop agency. It was focused on performance. What mattered most was whether students met scoring baselines and delivered output, not whether they understood or questioned anything. This wasn't for the students' benefit. It was for the schools, which rely on test results for funding and reputation. Critical thinking, reasoning, and reflection never had a real place in the system. As a result, students grow into adults who were never taught how to think for themselves or how to engage with the world on their own terms.

Now, with AI, that failure becomes *dangerous*. The technology will quietly and efficiently replace anyone who allows themselves to become interchangeable. It will not ask if you are capable. It will simply do the job.

And if you are not claiming your place in the process, you *will* be left out of it.

This is the hardest truth to face. People no longer have the option to wait for permission or instruction. They must learn to take agency, to think critically, to express judgment, to act with purpose, and above all, to take responsibility for their own decisions. AI will be helpful by design. It will also be indifferent. It will move forward either way.

The question is whether we will choose to participate, or whether we will quietly disappear.

Methodology

This book was developed with the structured support of *OpenAI's GPT-4o model*, used via ChatGPT between May and June 2025. GPT served as a research synthesis assistant and drafting partner throughout the process - summarizing academic sources, transforming raw insights into accessible narrative, and helping structure thematic arguments. The model did not generate standalone content; all direction, structuring, and refinement were driven by the author's editorial control, with iterative feedback and accuracy validation at each step. The use of AI was grounded in principles of transparency, augmentation, and intellectual accountability, consistent with the very framework the paper proposes: that AI should amplify human judgment - not replace it.

Acknowledgments

This book draws extensively on academic, policy, and nonprofit research published between 2022 and 2025 to illuminate the human, social, and civic implications of artificial intelligence. All referenced works are cited in the final References section and were reviewed in accordance with open-access availability, academic preprint standards, and institutional transparency. The synthesis presented here reflects an original narrative construction by the author, developed for civic, nonprofit, and public education purposes.

Dedication

To my girls, the loves of my life:
My wife, Sandra, and my daughters, Sarah and
Susanna.
I will always love you.
I wrote this for you - and for all the people I care for
deeply.

Contents

AI Orchestration Literacy: Quick Start Guide

AI orchestration is the skill of directing and refining AI output with purpose.

- You are not just *using* AI. You are *shaping* it.
- *You* decide what matters, and *You* guide the tool accordingly. Do *not* let AI decide for *You.*
- *You* tell AI what you need. And You will shape the output *together.*

Practice Prompts for Real Life

- *Help me start a conversation with my teenager about AI and responsible use.*
- *Draft a classroom policy for how students can use AI ethically and responsibly.*
- *Plan a simple 5-day promotion for my small business using email and social media.*

How to Work with AI Effectively

- *Ask clarifying or follow-up questions*
- *Challenge surprising claims*
- *Request step-by-step explanations*
- *Rephrase your prompt if the response feels incomplete*
- *Cross-check AI answers with trusted sources*

Final Reminder

- AI is a powerful tool, but *you* are the one directing it.
- Use it to *accelerate* your thinking. *Not to replace it.*

Three Core Prompt Patterns

Role + Task + Context

- Assign a Role + Define the Task + Provide Background.
  Act as a friendly marketing intern. Help me write a flyer for a library event aimed at parents.

Pareto Summary

- Ask for the most valuable ideas + **the 20% that matter most**.
  Summarize the most important points from this article using the Pareto Principle. Then explain them in clear, accessible language.

Bias and Clarity Check

- Use AI to evaluate information critically.
  Here's a paragraph I found online.
  Show me where it might be biased and rewrite it in a neutral, balanced way.

TL;DR (Too Long, Did Not Read)

You don't need credentials to teach orchestration. You don't need a title, a certificate, or permission.

What you need is presence. You need care. You need the willingness to step forward when others step back. You need agency: the kind that refuses to surrender the future to systems you had no hand in shaping.

Start small. Start at your kitchen table. Start at the library. Start with a friend who's uncertain about AI. Open a GPT session and say, *Let's try this together.* Then say, *Let's reflect on what it got right—and what it missed.* And most importantly, *Let's make sure we are not erased.*

If even that feels too big, start smaller. Share a story. Ask a question. Listen while someone works through their thoughts. Teach one person. Then let that person show someone else.

That's how it spreads. That's how it grows. Quietly, locally, deliberately. That's how we build fluency that belongs to everyone.

People say, *It is what it is.* But that's not true.

It will be what people decide.
With or without us.

A Glimpse of What's Possible

This is not speculation. It's a direction we can choose - but only if we learn to use AI with clarity and control. The future is not sealed; it is shaped by how we engage with these tools now. And if we get it right, here's what that future could look like.

Learning would become exponential. Students wouldn't turn to AI to do the work for them - they'd use it to accelerate their thinking, deepen their understanding, and explore on their own terms. Instant feedback would replace waiting. Personalized inquiry would replace standardized repetition.

This isn't about taking shortcuts. It's about cultivating minds that are sharper, more agile, and able to work alongside intelligence without being drowned by it.

Work would become more human, not less. The noise - the formatting, the scheduling, the status updates - would fall to the machine. What remains would be the part of work that can't be automated: the judgment, the ethics, the creativity, the care. Productivity would no longer mean burnout. It would mean focus. Purpose. Time spent on what matters.

The system would adapt to people, not the other way around. No more bending yourself to fit an algorithm. No more performance for machines.

Instead, we could design systems that respond to human intent - that invite direction rather than demand submission. People wouldn't just react to what AI generates. They would shape what it becomes.

Literacy would evolve. It would no longer be defined by reading, writing, or clicking. It would mean knowing how to ask a meaningful question, how to interpret a response, and how to guide the system that gave it.

We would move from passively consuming AI output to actively orchestrating it. From being told what's next to deciding what's next.

This future is not hypothetical. It is already possible - for those willing to engage. For those ready to learn how to stay human while working with machines. And for those who believe that presence, agency, and clarity still matter in a world of fluent simulation.

This Book is for You

This book isn't about AI hype. It's not about predicting the future or listing what jobs might disappear next. It's about something more immediate. It's about learning how to work with systems that are already here, already changing how we write, think, learn, and communicate.

Orchestration literacy means learning how to use AI with clarity and control. It's not a technical skill. It's not a job title. It's a new kind of basic literacy.

The ability to frame a problem, shape the output, and evaluate what comes back. If you don't have that ability, you'll be working inside systems you don't understand, doing tasks defined by tools you didn't choose. You will be assigned a series of tasks to perform and execute, without having the option to apply your own creativity, individuality and reasoning. You will be the *literal* cog in the machine.

But this isn't just about falling behind. It's also about what becomes possible when you learn to work with these tools deliberately.

This book exists because of that possibility. It wasn't just written about AI. It was written with AI. Every section, every paragraph, every revision involved collaboration between a human voice and a machine that can respond, restructure, and extend ideas in real time. That isn't a gimmick. It's orchestration in action. It changed what was possible for me, and it can do the same for you.

You don't need to become a machine learning expert. You don't need to memorize prompts or understand model weights. But you do need to engage. You do need to learn how to think with these systems instead of feeling overwhelmed by them. You will have to pay attention. Your future, our future, depends on it. I am serious.

This book is here to help you do that. Not to survive AI, but to use it well. Not to fear what's coming, but to take part in shaping it.

So take your time. Read carefully. What's in here is not just information. It's capability.

PART ONE:
The Wake-Up Call

The AI Disruption Is Already Here.

We are in the Future.

The Future is Here

Artificial Intelligence (AI) and automation are no longer futuristic concepts – they are actively reshaping jobs, businesses, and daily life in the United States.

Since 2022, rapid advances in generative AI have enabled machines to write code, draft legal documents, create art, and carry on conversations.

Major companies have rushed to deploy AI *copilots* and chatbots, boosting productivity but also reducing the need for certain roles. Small and medium-sized businesses face intense pressure to adopt these tools or risk falling behind more tech-savvy competitors.

Meanwhile, educational institutions struggle to update curricula fast enough to prepare students for an AI-driven world. Middle-class professional jobs – from office assistants to analysts – are under unprecedented strain as AI handles more cognitive tasks, potentially squeezing career opportunities. Companies often quietly restructure, using terms like *efficiency* and *augmentation* to mask workforce reductions due to AI.

The impacts are uneven, hitting some communities and demographics harder and raising concerns about mental health and regional inequalities. Based on tangible developments and investments through 2025, this report projects that by 2035 AI will be deeply embedded in most workplaces and households.

We can expect widespread deployment of AI assistants, further automation of routine work, and new job creation in tech – alongside growing calls for worker retraining, education reform, and thoughtful regulation to ensure this technological transformation benefits society as a whole.

In the past three years, breakthroughs in generative AI – algorithms that can produce human-like text, images, and even code – have gone from research labs to mainstream use virtually overnight. When OpenAI released ChatGPT in late 2022, it reached 100 million users within two months, the fastest adoption of any consumer application to date.

By 2024, millions of workers were incorporating tools like ChatGPT into daily tasks, from drafting emails to brainstorming ideas. Surveys found that roughly one in three U.S. workers had begun using AI on the job by 2024, a remarkable uptake for such a short period. Businesses across industries – finance, healthcare, law, manufacturing, retail – have launched pilot programs to automate workflows with AI.

In short, the future of work that experts have anticipated is rapidly becoming the present.

Current developments are *already* beginning to disrupt the world of work, business, and education, and what they portend for the coming decade. The sections that follow synthesize documented trends from 2022 through 2025, drawing on reputable studies and real cases.

From changes in everyday workplaces to broader societal impacts, you will see that AI-driven automation is not a hypothetical threat – it is *already* impacting job roles and economic landscapes.

Institutional Inertia

Regulation and Policy Landscape

Governments are waking up to the need for oversight of AI. This year the European Union began enforcing its AI Act, a comprehensive regulation that classifies AI systems by risk and imposes requirements like transparency and human oversight for higher-risk applications. This will likely affect U.S. companies that operate globally, effectively setting some standards here (for example, an American tech firm might decide to apply EU guidelines to its products worldwide for consistency).

In the U.S., while there is no single federal AI law yet, there are signs of movement. The White House issued an AI Bill of Rights framework in late 2023, which, among other things, pushed for safety testing of AI models and called for methods to watermark AI-generated content.

Workplace regulations may also evolve – for instance, requiring companies to consult workers or unions when introducing AI that could monitor performance or affect employment. Some states might implement their own rules. California, for example, has been active in considering laws about automated decision systems in employment.

Overall, regulation will likely lag technology, but by 2035 it should be firmly part of the AI landscape, shaping how companies deploy AI and giving individuals some recourse if AI is used in harmful ways.

Systemic Work Displacement

Changes in the World of Work

Work as we know it is being *profoundly altered* by AI technologies automating tasks that once required human effort. Entire categories of work are being augmented or even replaced by intelligent software. Specific role displacements have begun to emerge in offices and professional settings.

It is estimated that up to *70% - 100% of jobs will be impacted by Artificial Intelligence in the next 10 years*. Yes, you read this right. In short, *everyone will feel the impact of AI one way or another*.

Legal Services

In 2023, one of the world's largest law firms, Allen & Overy, deployed an AI legal assistant named Harvey to all 3,500 of its attorneys. Harvey and similar tools can draft contracts, scour documents for relevant case law, and even generate legal memos in seconds.

Associates traditionally billed many hours on such research and first-draft writing – tasks now streamlined by AI. While lawyers are not being summarily replaced, the firm's embrace of AI signals that fewer paralegals and junior lawyers may be needed for grunt work. Other firms quickly followed suit, and by 2024 dozens of major law offices were experimenting with AI in litigation and compliance work.

Legal professionals are learning to work alongside AI, reviewing and refining AI-produced drafts instead of writing from scratch.

Business Operations

Enterprise software providers have begun to embed AI-enabled components into day-to-day business tools. These systems are now standard in enterprise workflows. Tasks like data entry, basic accounting, and customer support are increasingly automated, reducing the need for roles once sustained by administrative repetition.

Creative and Content Work

Generative AI has made surprising inroads into creative domains. Marketing departments use tools like ChatGPT to produce first drafts of ad copy and social media posts. Publishers and media companies can have AI generate news summaries or sports recaps, reducing the need for entry-level writers.

Graphic design is also affected – tools can create logos, product mockups, or illustrations on demand, threatening freelance artist and designer jobs. Even in entertainment, AI voices and video generators are beginning to handle tasks like dubbing, basic animation, or background music composition.

Human creativity remains vital, but the volume of content that can be produced without a human involved in the creative process is unprecedented. In 2023, a major magazine acknowledged it had used AI to write dozens of online articles, with human editors polishing them. This sparked debate but also signaled how quickly content production workflows are changing.

AI Ubiquity in the Workplace

We can expect that many professionals will handle oversight and refinement of AI output rather than first-pass creation. For instance, a marketing coordinator in 2030 might have AI generate 10 slogan ideas and then choose the best one, rather than coming up with slogans from scratch. Productivity could soar, but so could expectations for output, since one person can do much more with AI help.

The role of human workers will increasingly center on what AI cannot do well alone: strategic decision-making, complex problem-solving, deep interpersonal communication, and creative innovation that requires cross-domain knowledge or genuine empathy.

New Job Creation and Transformation

Even as certain jobs disappear, new roles will emerge related to AI. Already we've seen demand for machine learning engineers, data scientists, and AI ethicists. By 2035, there will be whole categories we're only beginning to imagine: AI auditors (professionals who check AI systems for bias or errors), prompt engineers (specialists in crafting effective inputs to AI models – though interestingly, some predict this role will itself be temporary as AI gets better at understanding intent), robot maintenance technicians for the next generation of service robots, virtual environment designers (if AI and augmented reality converge for training and entertainment), and many more.

Existing jobs will also take on new dimensions – a teacher in 2035 might routinely use AI to personalize lesson plans for each student, requiring skill in managing AI educational software. A doctor might work with AI diagnostic tools and need to be as much a data analyst as a medical expert.

While automation will reduce headcount in some traditional roles, it will also create value and jobs in others. Importantly, the new jobs will generally require higher levels of digital literacy and adaptability, which circles back to the educational reforms needed that were discussed earlier. Acquiring orchestration literacy is crucial.

Physical Automation and AI in Daily Life

While much of the AI disruption has been in digital and cognitive tasks, the coming decade will likely bring AI into the physical world at scale.

Multiple companies are investing in autonomous vehicles – it's plausible that by the early 2030s, self-driving taxis and delivery trucks will be operating in many U.S. cities. Major logistics firms are already testing driverless long-haul trucks in the Southwest; if those trials meet safety and cost targets, long-distance trucking jobs could diminish by 2035, with human drivers focusing on last-mile or supervisory roles.

In retail and food service, we'll see more cashier-less stores and more kitchen automation, such as robotic cooks and automated beverage dispensers. This doesn't mean humans vanish from these industries, but a single person might oversee several automated systems.

Continued Acceleration and Investment

One reason these changes will keep advancing is the enormous and growing investment in AI. Tech companies collectively invested tens of billions of dollars into AI research and startups from 2022 to 2025. Venture capital funding for AI tools, government research grants – all are at all-time highs. Notably, Microsoft's multibillion-dollar partnership with OpenAI, Google's heavy R&D spending on AI (including its DeepMind division), Amazon's $4 billion investment in Anthropic (another AI lab), and numerous other deals guarantee that AI capabilities will continue to improve.

We are likely to see more powerful AI models (perhaps GPT-5 or beyond) in this timeframe, with better reasoning, more reliability, and multimodal abilities (seamlessly handling images, speech, and text). Such models could broaden the range of tasks AI can do – maybe tackling more creative endeavors or more sensitive decision-making that current AIs struggle with. Committed corporate roadmaps also suggest AI will be integrated in critical infrastructure: think AI managing power grids for efficiency, AI helping run smart cities (traffic control, public safety monitoring), and AI in defense (autonomous drones or cybersecurity systems).

By 2035, AI might be as commonplace and unremarkable as electricity is today – embedded everywhere, largely invisible until something goes wrong.

Small and Medium Businesses Are Under Pressure

For America's 30 million small and mid-sized businesses, AI is a double-edged sword.

On one hand, accessible AI tools promise big efficiency gains and a chance to compete with larger firms. On the other, many smaller businesses lack the resources or know-how to fully leverage AI, potentially leaving them behind. The past two years have seen a surge in AI awareness among small business owners, along with mounting pressure to adopt these technologies or risk obsolescence.

Surveys in 2023–2024 revealed a striking uptick in AI uptake by smaller companies. In early 2024 the U.S. Chamber of Commerce reported that 40% of small businesses said they were using generative AI tools, nearly double the share (23%) from just a year prior. These AI-adopting businesses aren't tech startups in Silicon Valley, but everyday enterprises – local retailers, restaurants, marketing agencies, consultants – that have started integrating AI into operations.

For example, a neighborhood bakery might use an AI tool to manage inventory and predict demand, reducing waste. A family-run real estate office might deploy a chatbot on its website to answer customer questions after hours. A boutique marketing firm can have copywriting AI draft client blog posts, allowing it to serve more clients with the same staff. Small manufacturers are beginning to use AI-driven robots or quality control systems once reserved for industry giants.

In theory, AI is an equalizer, allowing lean businesses to punch above their weight. Yet, this optimistic narrative has a flip side.

Many small and medium businesses (SMBs) are struggling to keep up. Implementing AI isn't as simple as flipping a switch – it requires investment, data, and skills that smaller firms may not have.

A U.S. Census analysis found that in late 2023, the smallest businesses (under 5 employees) did start adopting generative AI at a notable rate, but overall AI usage still scales with firm size. Large enterprises (250+ employees) tend to have dedicated IT teams and budgets to experiment with AI, whereas a ten-person company might not even know where to begin. Concerns about cost, cybersecurity, and the reliability of AI outputs hold some owners back.

There is also a growing gap between early adopters and laggards in the SMB space: some firms are diving in and reaping benefits, while others haven't touched the technology. This divide could exacerbate competition, with tech-forward local businesses pulling ahead of those that remain analog.

Moreover, even when small businesses adopt AI, it can be disruptive to their workforce and ways of working. If a small medical office introduces an AI system to handle patient scheduling and billing, the front-desk staff might find their roles diminished or require new training to oversee the system.

Small firms often operate like families, with employees wearing multiple hats – introducing automation can be culturally jolting. Owners may face tough choices about whether to let go of loyal employees when an AI solution could handle the work instead.

Under pressure aptly describes the situation for SMBs: pressure to adopt AI to stay efficient, pressure on employees who fear being replaced, and pressure on owners to navigate the financial and ethical complexities of this transition.

Looking ahead, most small businesses are expected to integrate some form of AI by the end of the decade, through software-as-a-service platforms, smart devices, or embedded automation. Those that successfully blend human touch with AI efficiency could thrive against larger competitors. Those that don't may see margins shrink or customers drift toward more automated alternatives. At the same time, large enterprises face pressure of their own, racing to stay nimble as smaller, AI-native challengers threaten to outpace them.

The playing field is shifting, and the next section turns to whether our educational systems are keeping pace in preparing the workforce of tomorrow for this new reality.

From Output to Action: The Rise of Agents

Generative AI no longer just produces content, it executes. Autonomous agents can now read instructions, browse the web, write and run code, submit forms, or even interact with other systems in real time. They don't wait for approval. They act. It can switch job roles at the push of a button, from researcher to recruiter to salesperson, without asking if the job is still needed, or if it should exist at all.

The AI Chasm in Education

Education's Mismatch with Reality

While industry hurtles forward with AI, the U.S. education system is scrambling to catch up – and largely falling behind. There is a growing mismatch between what schools and colleges are teaching and the skills that the AI-driven economy demands. Curricula, accreditation standards, and career guidance often reflect yesterday's job market more than tomorrow's, leaving students ill-prepared for a world where automation is ubiquitous.

One stark example can be found in Georgia's official career planning materials.

The state's *Hot Careers to 2032* list, marketed to high school students as stable and high paying, includes roles like accountant, data analyst, lawyer, and even commercial pilot. Yet many of these same jobs are also among the most vulnerable to AI disruption. This is a contradiction that reflects how slowly career guidance is adapting to reality.

This isn't to say those careers will vanish – but their trajectories and skill requirements are changing fast. Unfortunately, educational curricula often haven't adapted. In fact, curriculum lag is evident at multiple levels.

K-12 Schools

In April 2025, the federal government issued orders to expand AI education in K–12. The directive mandates federal agencies to work with states in making AI-focused courses and certificate programs available in high schools, aiming to equip students with foundational literacy in AI tools and concepts. While a promising signal, the policy remains at early stages of implementation, and widespread integration into state curricula may lag behind the technology's pace.

Computer science and AI-related courses are still absent from many schools. While coding classes have slowly expanded, few districts teach *AI literacy* – how machine learning works, ethical implications, or how to use AI tools effectively.

Students might graduate high school having never interacted with an AI beyond perhaps a voice assistant on their phone. Core subjects like math and reading remain crucial, but there is little integration of AI topics into mainstream learning.

Meanwhile, technologies like ChatGPT have upended traditional assignments (with students using AI to write essays, and teachers unsure how to respond). Rather than updating teaching methods or curricula, many schools defaulted to banning AI use, which does little to prepare students for responsible usage in college or work.

Higher Education

Universities are turning out graduates in fields that may be saturated or transformed by automation.

For example, many colleges have encouraged booming enrollment in computer science and data science programs – yet these programs often focus on classical programming and analysis techniques, not on how to collaborate with AI coding assistants or verify AI-driven insights.

Business schools teach management and finance with cases from the pre-AI era, even as MBA graduates now find workplaces where AI plays an assistant manager role (e.g. for analyzing reports, suggesting decisions).

Law schools still largely rely on traditional legal research training, though by graduation students may join firms using AI for first-pass research.

Even vocational and technical education is behind; trades like auto mechanics or medical technicians are quickly incorporating AI diagnostics, but training programs are only beginning to mention those.

The result is graduates who may have strong foundational knowledge but lack practical experience with the AI tools that are becoming standard in their fields.

Risk for the classes of 2030 and beyond

The risks for the classes of 2030 and beyond is that they enter a workforce in which many *safe* occupations have been radically redefined. If education does not align with reality, young people may find themselves needing extensive retraining early in their careers.

We also must acknowledge that students and parents may be making life-shaping decisions based on outdated expectations. A student might pursue a degree in pharmacy or radiology, fields known for good employment prospects, not realizing that AI is making rapid inroads into reading medical images and dispensing medications.

Or consider the emphasis on promoting STEM (science, technology, engineering, math) careers; it's well-intentioned, but even within STEM, the specific skills in demand are shifting. For instance, knowing how to prompt and validate an AI system might become as important as knowing how to manually code an algorithm. Yet few are explicitly taught that. 2030's graduates could emerge with skills for jobs that no longer exist, while jobs that do exist, like AI ethicist or robot technician, have few training pipelines.

There are efforts underway to bridge this gap – several universities in 2024 introduced interdisciplinary AI courses for all students, and some K-12 districts have piloted AI ethics modules. But systemic change is slow. The inertia in updating textbooks, exams, and teacher training contrasts sharply with the breakneck pace of AI advancement.

Meanwhile, the very existence of AI raises questions about what skills humans should prioritize. Creativity, critical thinking, adaptability, and empathy – these uniquely human skills become more important when AI handles the routine parts. Yet standardized tests and admission criteria seldom measure or incentivize those.

In sum, there is a serious misalignment: educational institutions are promoting career paths and teaching skills for a world that is fast disappearing, unless they urgently adapt to the presence of AI in every industry.

The Collapse of Agency

Misusing AI to Bypass Learning

While some learners have embraced GPT tools to deepen understanding, clarify dense concepts, or simulate feedback from a mentor, others use the same systems to bypass learning altogether. Term papers are drafted in seconds, quiz answers are copy-pasted from chat transcripts, and take-home exams become exercises in prompt engineering, not comprehension. What was once framed as *studying smarter* can, without any guardrails or reflection, devolve into the *mass outsourcing of cognition*.

Academic institutions were unprepared for the sudden ubiquity of generative AI. Rubrics stayed static while the reality of authorship changed overnight.

The result is a hollowing-out of trust. Professors second-guess every essay. Peers who did the work feel resentful. And learners who relied too heavily on GPT often can't explain, much less defend, what they turned in.

Worse, some students convince themselves they're being pragmatic. They're *just keeping up* they say, as deadlines multiply and the pressure to perform intensifies. AI becomes the crutch that slowly atrophies the very muscles it promised to support. This is not *augmentation*. It's an *unraveling*.

A recent study titled *Brain on GPT: Cognitive Effects of Language Models on Human Thinking* provides compelling empirical support for the central thesis of this book. The researchers found that exposure to GPT-4 not only shifts users' beliefs - even on controversial topics - but also reduces cognitive effort, induces answer alignment with the model (even when it is incorrect), and erodes confidence in one's own reasoning. Participants reported that GPT responses *sounded smarter than me*, illustrating a subtle but powerful authority transfer from human to machine. This ambient influence occurred without any persuasive intent, suggesting that LLMs can reshape cognition simply by being consulted.

The result is a convergence of thinking, loss of originality, and passive acceptance - especially among users lacking critical scaffolding. These findings underscore the urgent need for orchestration literacy: without deliberate intervention, language models risk becoming cognitive replacements rather than amplifiers. This book proposes a different path: One where humans remain the orchestrators, not the instruments.

Identity and Class Compression

Cognitive Middle-Class Compression

One of the most unsettling impacts of the current AI wave is on the mid-skill, mid-income tier of jobs – essentially, the cognitive middle class of the workforce.

These are roles that require significant knowledge and judgment but also involve a lot of routine information processing: think of office managers, mid-level analysts, technicians, customer service supervisors, HR specialists, and many roles in sales, finance, and healthcare administration.

Traditionally, such white-collar jobs have been the backbone of the middle class. Now they face what might be called a *compression*, as AI automation hollows out many of the repetitive duties that justified junior and mid-level positions.

Generative AI is moving up the skill chain in ways the public is only starting to grasp.

For decades, automation primarily threatened jobs that were manual or repetitive – assembly line workers, bank tellers, grocery cashiers. Those changes were significant but often created new demand for higher-skilled jobs managing or programming the machines.

Today's AI is different. It can analyze, converse, and create, which means it targets jobs that involve sitting at a computer handling information – jobs held by millions of Americans with college degrees.

For example, an AI has no issues to:
- sift through thousands of pages of documents to extract key points - something a team of paralegals or junior consultants might do
- generate a detailed marketing strategy or a project plan draft - tasks a marketing associate or project manager would handle
- provide a first cut at a scientific literature review or an insurance claim assessment.

These are tasks that used to secure the employment of many entry and mid-level professionals. A recent Pew

Research Center survey highlighted this shift: the public and AI experts both believe that white-collar, process-oriented jobs are highly exposed to AI.

This exposure doesn't guarantee replacement; it does mean these jobs will be deeply changed. Researchers from Brookings Institution have noted that office and administrative support roles are among the most vulnerable, given they involve structured tasks that AI excels at, such as scheduling, bookkeeping or form-filling.

Indeed, the World Economic Forum forecasts roughly 26 million fewer administrative jobs globally by 2027 as companies deploy automated systems in those functions. These were solid middle-class positions that provided livelihoods across the country, from big cities to small towns.

For example, AI chatbots and voice assistants can handle routine inquiries in customer service, so one human agent can oversee multiple AI interactions rather than directly serving each customer – leading companies to need fewer agents on staff. Even in management, there is a trend toward flatter organizations as AI decision-support tools allow senior managers to oversee more subordinates effectively, potentially squeezing out layers of middle management.

The net effect is a possible polarization of the workforce. High-skill jobs that involve complex strategy, cutting-edge research, or specialized expertise (often requiring advanced degrees) will remain in demand and perhaps even become more productive alongside AI. And many lower-skill jobs that require physical presence or personal interaction are less directly affected by AI in the near term.

But a broad swath of middle-tier cognitive jobs could shrink in number or in relative compensation. If an AI can handle 60% of a research analyst's tasks, a company might employ fewer analysts or hire less at entry-level and focus on a smaller number of strategists to interpret AI outputs. The worry is a compression of middle-class career pathways: fewer rungs on the ladder, and possibly stagnant wages, as the economic value of those intermediate skills declines. There are already reports as of June 2025 that the so-called 'first rung' of the career ladder that represents entry-level jobs has already started to disappear.

In concrete terms, an economic analysis by Goldman Sachs in 2023 estimated that as many as two-thirds of U.S. occupations could have a significant portion of their tasks automated by AI in the coming decade. They noted that most jobs will be partially, not fully, automated – meaning humans will still work in those fields, but the nature of the work changes.

Without intervention, the trend points toward a challenging landscape for mid-career professionals who expected steady advancement but now must compete with algorithms doing substantial portions of their jobs.

Mental Health and Anxiety

On an individual level, the specter of AI-related job insecurity is causing stress. Polls show most U.S. workers are now worried that AI could threaten their livelihood. In one 2024 survey by a major consulting firm, 71% of employees expressed concern that AI will negatively impact their job security, and two in five felt AI advancements were happening too fast for comfort.

This pervasive anxiety – sometimes dubbed *AI anxiety* – can take a mental health toll. Workers may feel pressure to constantly upskill, prove their worth beyond the machine, or simply cope with the uncertainty of not knowing if their role will exist in a few years. According to mental health professionals, chronic workplace anxiety of this kind can lead to burnout, decreased job performance, and general life stress.

Unfortunately, because AI changes are often subtle or unspoken (the *silent* aspect discussed earlier), employees might be worrying in a vacuum, without clear communication from employers about what to expect. That can make the anxiety worse.

A May 2025 report highlighted that AI-related workplace anxiety is not just anecdotal - it's statistically significant and rising. With mounting concerns about job stability and role obsolescence, workers are experiencing heightened stress. The report urged employers to implement proactive mental health programs as a core part of their AI adaptation strategies.

For younger people who are just entering the workforce or still in school, anxiety also looms. This anticipation of a more competitive, automated job market can manifest as chronic stress about the future. Career uncertainty joins other modern stressors (like climate change or societal unrest) in weighing on young people's minds.

Mental health professionals note that having a coherent sense of identity and future direction is crucial for adolescents' psychological development; when the future of work seems unpredictable, it can hinder youths' ability to form that healthy identity. They might feel, *What's the point of my education if a robot will do my job?* or internalize a narrative of humans being *less than* or replaceable, which can be demoralizing.

The Threat of Identity Foreclosure

At the same time, millions of workers in their 30s, 40s, and 50s – many of them parents – are confronting the reality that the careers they have built might radically change. Layoffs in industries undergoing automation, such as manufacturing, customer service or retail, can lead to what psychologists call *identity foreclosure*: when a defining role or status, like being the family breadwinner is lost, individuals often experience grief akin to *losing a part of themselves.*

Work is a primary source of self-esteem and social belonging for many adults. As one Harvard Business Review article succinctly put it, *work provides recognition, status, and reinforcement of our self-concept* – so losing a job can shatter one's sense of identity and well-being. Even the anticipation of potential job loss can cause chronic anxiety and a feeling of helplessness, which may spill over into family life.

Fallout and Disparity

Communities and People Are Left Behind

The consequences of AI-driven disruption are not being felt equally by everyone. Just as previous economic shifts like globalization, or the decline of manufacturing, created winners and losers across different regions and groups, the rise of AI is producing an uneven impact. Understanding who is most affected – and how – is crucial for addressing the societal strain that technology can impose.

Community-Level Disparities

Certain communities, especially those economically reliant on a few key employers or industries, are vulnerable to AI upheaval.

We're essentially seeing a parallel to what happened in factory towns, but now in office parks and service centers. Regions that built economies around routine white-collar work – call centers, data processing hubs, administrative offices – could become the new *rust belt* as AI automates those functions.

By contrast, major tech hubs and diversified urban economies might absorb AI changes more fluidly, even gaining jobs in AI development and deployment. This creates a geographical disparity: metropolitan areas with innovation industries may thrive, while smaller cities or rural areas with more automatable roles struggle. The result can be increased internal migration as workers leave hard-hit areas, and greater regional inequality.

Sven D. Olensky

Labor Market Segmentation

AI is also affecting demographic groups differently. Workers with higher education and digital skills are generally better positioned to adapt or move into new roles created by AI. Those with less education, who often filled many of the administrative and support roles now at risk, may find it harder to secure good jobs if their positions are cut.

There are concerns that historically disadvantaged groups could be hit harder. For instance, analysis by McKinsey and others indicates Black and Hispanic workers in the U.S. are overrepresented in certain occupations at high-risk of AI replacement, such as support roles in customer service, healthcare, and retail cashiers. If those jobs decline, these communities might face disproportionate job loss, exacerbating racial economic gaps.

Similarly, older workers may find it more challenging to retrain in AI-centric skills if their jobs are automated, potentially accelerating early retirements or long-term unemployment among the 50+ age group. We could see a scenario where younger, tech-savvy workers adapt and flourish while some older colleagues are left behind – a form of generational disparity.

Uneven Access to Opportunities

The benefits of AI (such as new jobs or increased productivity) will not be evenly distributed. High-tech industries and well-capitalized companies, often in coastal cities or innovation hubs, are creating many of the AI developer and engineer roles – and those typically require advanced degrees or specialized training. Not everyone can tap into those opportunities.

Even within a company, AI might help boost profitability, but if that leads mostly to gains for shareholders or top executives while front-line workers are cut, inequality widens. Some economists warn that without intervention, AI could further concentrate wealth and income, as those who design and manage AI reap outsized rewards compared to those whose jobs are made redundant.

We also see uneven impact globally that touches the U.S. indirectly. For example, countries like India and the Philippines have largely outsourced service sectors that are at risk from AI-driven chatbot and process automation. If those jobs decline, it can cause instability or migration pressures that eventually affect global markets and communities, including diaspora communities in the U.S.

Conversely, some countries investing heavily in AI education and infrastructure might surge ahead economically. The U.S. must compete with those developments as well, but within the country, certain states or cities investing in AI training could get a leg up, while others fall behind.

Across all these examples, roles are not necessarily being eliminated overnight, but their nature is shifting. Workers find themselves supervising AI outputs, handling exceptions, and focusing on higher-level judgment and interpersonal tasks while the AI takes care of the repetitive groundwork. Still, fewer hands may be required for that groundwork.

Community leaders and policymakers are beginning to take note. Unions have started to negotiate about AI in contracts, aiming to secure re-training programs or protections against job loss due to technology.

Some local governments in regions heavily impacted by automation are seeking to attract new types of employers or invest in tech education to create alternative pathways. Mental health professionals are urging companies to be transparent and provide support to employees facing AI changes, to mitigate stress.

These responses are only in the early stages. The uneven impacts of AI, if left unaddressed, could deepen divisions - between urban and rural, skilled and less-skilled, younger and older, majority and minority.

Ensuring a more equitable outcome will likely require conscious effort: in distributing AI's productivity gains, in retraining workers, in supporting affected communities, and in preparing every segment of society for the changes underway.

Projecting into the next decade, we must base expectations on concrete developments already in motion: corporate roadmaps, announced investments, and regulatory plans. Assuming no major reversals, by 2035 AI and automation will be even more pervasive in work, education, and daily life.

Societal Adjustments

The next decade may well bring contentious debates about the role of AI. We could see movements advocating for a shorter work week or universal basic income if job displacement becomes acute – ideas to distribute the productivity gains of AI more broadly.

Education will likely undergo reforms under pressure; by 2035 more schools might include AI training, and lifelong learning could become the norm as mid-career workers regularly cycle through re-skilling programs. Culturally, there will be ongoing negotiation of AI's place – for instance, in art and media, questions about authenticity of AI-generated content may lead to new norms, or at least new genres.

Issues of bias and fairness in AI decisions, like who gets approved for a loan or hired for a job by an AI filter, will probably lead to standards and audits as routine practice. Many of these changes are being discussed now in 2025 and pilot programs are starting; by 2035, they could be standard operating procedure.

In summary, barring an unexpected *AI winter* or backlash, the momentum of current investments and initiatives means that AI will be deeply interwoven into the fabric of everyday life and work by 2035.

We will likely look back on 2025 the way one might look back on the early days of the internet – recognizing it as the start of a sea change, but marveling at how much further it evolved in a short time. The challenge and opportunity before us will require us to channel this evolution in ways that enhance human well-being and address the disruptions highlighted in this report, rather than simply letting change wash over society unchecked.

Good Enough:
A Nightmare Scenario

Across a growing number of industries, workers are now required - or strongly pressured - to use generative AI tools as a condition of staying competitive. AI is no longer marketed just as an accelerator of productivity. It is becoming a measure of performance. In some cases, usage is tracked, reviewed, and discussed as part of formal evaluation. Workers are expected to demonstrate engagement with AI tools routinely, regardless of whether those tools improve process or outcome.

What began as a promise of augmentation is quickly becoming a framework of coercion. This shift is particularly harmful to professions grounded in creativity, authorship, interpretation, or judgment: design, writing, analysis, policy development, curriculum creation, communications, and other cognitive disciplines. These roles depend not on repetition or scale, but on insight, timing, and careful discernment.

AI tools, by contrast, are optimized for speed, surface coherence, and fast content generation. Once in the workflow, they redefine what is considered a normal pace of output.

A task that may have previously involved one draft and two iterations can now yield ten variations in a matter of minutes. That new potential becomes the new expectation. Workers are no longer judged only on the quality of their contributions but on their ability to demonstrate visible productivity through tool use.

If AI can generate five options, why did you only bring one?

That question now appears across nearly every profession where quality once justified time.

In marketing, a campaign story that would have taken a team ten days - refining voice, pacing, and message - is now expected in a fraction of that time. The system can generate a batch of headlines in under a minute. The result may lack alignment or depth, but it appears complete. Review cycles are skipped. The process is overruled.

In product design, what once required weeks of iteration - sketching, visual refinement, material tradeoffs - is now replaced by dozens of image outputs generated in seconds. It does not matter if they are structurally viable. They look like deliverables. That is often enough.

In consulting, a strategic framework that might have involved five days of interviews, synthesis, and alignment work is now challenged by instant outputs. *You could have prompted a few templates and refined from there.* The baseline has shifted. The signal of effort is now quantity.

In curriculum development, differentiated lesson plans that once required careful scaffolding and alignment to developmental benchmarks are now expected on demand. Systems can generate beginner, intermediate, and advanced versions instantly. The underlying structure is rarely examined.

In legal, contract language once drafted slowly and deliberately is now expected to begin with multiple system-generated clauses. These may be inconsistent or risky, but the burden of judgment remains with the human while the time allowed to apply it continues to shrink.

In technical writing and research, a single abstract is no longer sufficient. The expectation is to produce multiple rewrites, even when the original is correct. Variation becomes a proxy for rigor. Review is replaced by comparison.

And in creative work - writing, music, film - the shift is absolute. Scenes, choruses, treatments that once took days of emotional and structural iteration are now expected in volume. The assumption is that a tool can generate enough starting points that the human can simply choose.

The shift is not only about speed. It is about *substitution*. Simulated effort becomes indistinguishable from real process. What took a week of thinking can now be rendered in one minute - and that becomes the new expectation.

This is *simulation shock*, operationalized. It is not presented as a disruption. It is presented as normal. And once the baseline moves, the burden of justification shifts *entirely to the worker*.

This logic reframes the entire nature of creative labor. It shifts the value proposition from thoughtful creation to rapid thoughtful generation.

Yet generative tools are far from frictionless. They frequently introduce factual errors, stylistic inconsistencies, brand misalignments, citation issues, or structural problems that are not always visible at first glance. Workers who rely on these systems must absorb the burden of verification, correction, and postprocessing. In many organizations, this corrective labor is not formally recognized or accounted for.

This pattern unfolds predictably. A worker uses AI to meet increased productivity expectations. The tool generates outputs that are plausible but flawed, introducing errors or structural issues that require revision.

The worker, now functioning as a last-mile quality layer, must correct the output under deadline. The time spent on cleanup is invisible to leadership, yet performance metrics continue to rise. Over time, output expectations compound, while support, discretion, and recognition decline. The result is a measurable deterioration in both productivity and morale.

This loop is not confined to any one role. Designers find themselves correcting off-brand layouts. Writers spend more time rewriting AI-generated drafts than if they had written from scratch. Analysts must verify hallucinated citations and inconsistent data. Each of these workers becomes responsible for delivering a final product that looks efficient from a distance but carries the invisible labor of repair.

When usage itself becomes a performance metric, the space to push back collapses. Workers are discouraged from ignoring or rejecting flawed outputs, even when doing so would improve quality.

Compliance with the system becomes more important than discretion. The more these dynamics take hold, the more the creative process is flattened into a performance of obedience.

The emotional consequences are significant. Workers begin to experience anticipatory stress - not just about the volume of work required, but about whether the tools they are required to use will silently fail them.

Most are not trained in the internal behaviors of large language models. They are not told how or why outputs hallucinate, degrade, or vary with prompt context. They are held responsible for the quality of something they do not fully control but are nevertheless expected to deliver from.

Institutional decision-makers, particularly those in upper management, are often unaware of the technical and psychological dynamics at play. They are sold on AI's potential to improve efficiency, reduce headcount, and accelerate decision-making.

But they are not exposed to the time spent validating outputs, the strain of error correction, or the downstream risk of acting on faulty results. Vendors rarely communicate these limitations clearly, and so a gap opens up between what leadership believes the tool is doing and what workers must do to make its output usable.

This is not *augmentation* in any meaningful sense. It is a reframing of creative work as a series of extractable interactions. The goal becomes speed. The method becomes tool dependency. The result is a form of industrialization applied not to physical labor, but to judgment, tone, timing, and authorship. What was once protected by expertise is now open to override by volume metrics.

In truth, leadership has rarely prioritized quality in the ways workers often assume. Enterprise delivery culture is structured around timelines, client demands, budget tradeoffs, and minimum viable products.

These terms formalize what many professionals already know: the goal is not excellence. The goal is delivery that holds together under pressure, looks presentable from a distance, and survives executive review. Over time, these constraints were normalized. Workers adapted.

What changed was not the priority. What changed was who does the work.

Historically, professionals operated within this constraint by threading the needle. They found ways to inject care, fix flaws, and deliver more than was strictly required. This labor was never tracked or incentivized, but it is what made organizations sustainable.

It is what allowed products to feel considered, services to feel human, and documents to feel like they were written by someone who *actually cared*. That informal layer of care is now under threat.

AI-generated output delivers exactly what many systems have long optimized for: plausible structure, minimum friction, and acceptable results at scale. The alignment is not accidental. It is structural. AI delivers minimum viable content at enterprise speed - and for many decision-makers, that is not a compromise. *It is the ideal.*

What is being lost is not polish. It is *ownership*. It is the ability to shape a thing beyond its spec. To say, *This is not ready,* and be taken seriously. When AI becomes the baseline for MVPs, workers are no longer seen as experts. They are seen as blockers.

This is not a breakdown in tooling. It is the collapse of a decades-old contract between leadership and those who were trusted to care even when no one asked them to. Professionals did not work this way because they were told to. They did it because the work *mattered*.

The result is not just burnout. It is *erosion*. The internal reference point begins to drift. People begin to question whether their standards are outdated. Whether anyone notices. Whether anyone cares.

And this is where the damage deepens. Because the fix to this dynamic is not more training. It is not more efficient prompting. It is not a better interface. Those may help temporarily, but they do not change the structural reality: *creative work is being compressed into a delivery model that cannot sustain the psychological, intellectual, or ethical frameworks that once gave it meaning.*

The Pipeline of Compliance

This transformation does not begin in the workplace. It begins in school.

More and more students are using generative tools not because they were instructed to, but because they can. Faced with deadlines, unclear expectations, and high-stakes testing, they reach for systems that promise faster results and higher scores. And in many cases, they succeed - at least on paper.

The response from educational institutions has been cautious, conflicted, and uneven. On the surface, many schools and colleges warn against misuse. But beneath the policies, there is an unspoken tension: if generative tools help students raise their scores, then institutional performance metrics improve as well. Graduation rates climb. Average test scores rise. Application pipelines grow. Rankings stabilize.

No one has to say it directly. But the incentives are clear: *if the output improves, why would the system push back?*

This creates a quiet, mutual accommodation: students disengage from the process of thinking, and institutions do not challenge the illusion of mastery. Everyone benefits - *except the student, who begins to lose the thread of authorship before adulthood ever begins.*

What starts as convenience becomes *dependence*. The ability to generate ten essay drafts in seconds trains a reflex: produce, scan, submit, forget. Judgment erodes. Confidence collapses. But deliverables remain high, and the system keeps moving.

By the time these students enter the workforce, they are already adapted. They know how to meet a target. They know how to generate *plausible* output. They know how to move quickly and not ask too many questions. They have been rewarded for performance, not process.

From school to workplace, the message is consistent:
Creativity is optional. Compliance is not.
Deliver, and you are safe.
Deviate, and you are a problem.

This is not a failure of the students. It is a structural handoff between two systems that both benefit from *appearances*. A handoff between institutions that claim to develop minds and institutions that demand deliverables. The result is a generation of workers trained not in discernment or originality, but in the art of being *good enough*.

Conclusion

There is no immediate remedy. The system is not designed for reversal. The incentives are aligned toward acceleration, standardization, and throughput. Workers and students cannot opt out individually. They are being pushed into a realignment that redefines their role - not as creators, but as output managers.

This book does not promise a solution. It cannot reverse what is already underway. But it can offer a place to begin: a framework for naming what is happening, and for preserving what can still be defended.

The system may no longer prioritize integrity. But the choice to defend it, quietly or visibly, remains ours to make.

Because when this erosion is no longer questioned - when simulated output becomes indistinguishable from effort - what happens next is not just professional collapse.

It is personal dislocation. The unraveling of authorship. The dulling of presence. The quiet crisis that arrives without announcement.

This is the moment we call *Simulation Shock*. And this is where we go next.

Interlude:
Simulation Shock

We are not prepared for this. Nobody is.

But we must face it.

Humanity depends on it.

Demonstrating the Shock

Demonstrate simulation shock by describing common job roles in detail, without needing any context. Show how deeply you understand each role's tasks, tools, and mindset by default - then include a final example of what AI agents can already do to emphasize that no one is safe.

Factory Worker (Manufacturing Plant)

Arrives early to suit up - protective gear checked, boots laced, badge scanned. Heads to assigned station on the floor. Could be welding, operating a lathe, inspecting parts with calipers, or loading pallets for parts flow. Follows production cadence closely - knows when something is off by the sound of the line. Reports issues through the floor escalation system.

Communicates directly with maintenance when equipment starts drifting. Tracks output against efficiency metrics. Complies with every safety protocol without thinking - because not doing so gets people hurt. Lunch break is short, precise. Final hour is cleanup, reset, and quality checks. Never leaves early, always knows when volume is behind.

HR Manager

Starts by checking pending approvals, employee flags, or unresolved cases. Reviews candidate pipeline and interviews scheduled for the day. Drafts documentation for a coaching conversation scheduled with a frontline manager. Joins a leadership meeting to discuss workforce planning. Tracks headcount data against budget. Flags a pattern of exits in one team. Reviews anonymous feedback from recent surveys. Updates policy language for compliance with new labor guidelines. Schedules a training session on unconscious bias. Balances legal risk, emotional nuance, and internal politics. Understands where the culture is starting to fray - often before anyone says it out loud.

VP of Finance

Opens the day reviewing updated numbers - variance reports, cash flow, forecasts. Investigates discrepancies in cost allocations. Questions an unexpected uptick in expenses tied to a product launch. Reviews capital expenditures against annual targets. Works with the team on next-quarter modeling, adjusting for revenue shifts and cost headwinds.

Prepares materials for an upcoming review with the board. Analyzes performance across business units. Signs off on a few large vendor payments, rejecting one due to contract misalignment. Focused not just on dollars, but on patterns - spending trends, margin erosion, operational risk. Keeps the company solvent, but more than that, keeps it from drifting.

Chief Technology Officer (CTO)

Checks overnight alerts from engineering leads. Starts with a morning sync - key topics include platform reliability, delayed deployments, and a looming audit gap in infrastructure. Discusses risk mitigation for data access controls. Reviews an internal proposal for architecture overhaul. Approves staffing plan to scale a new product team. Meets with legal and security on AI system governance.

Pushes back on vendor pitch that lacks clarity on model behavior and data boundaries. Balances performance, cost, and long-term sustainability. Thinks five systems ahead, across stacks and silos. Understands both the elegance of the solution and the mess behind the scenes. Never confuses uptime with health.

Chief Executive Officer (CEO)

Starts day reviewing the exec summary deck - P&L trends, headcount, key risk indicators, customer churn, legal exposure. Has a standing one-on-one with the CFO (cash position, debt structure), COO (supply chain volatility, fulfillment bottlenecks), and CPO (employee sentiment from pulse surveys, Glassdoor deltas). Preps for investor meeting - must thread the needle between innovation narrative and cost discipline.

Reviews Net Promoter Score dips, correlates to last quarter's pricing changes. Debriefs with General Counsel on pending litigation. Speaks with lead independent director about succession pipeline and whistleblower tip. Lives in narrative control, strategic hedging, stakeholder triage. Knows that every word spoken can move stock price, morale, and retention.

State Senator

Starts with constituent call summaries - housing complaint, zoning dispute, Medicaid rejection. Reviews overnight legislative alerts: three bills moving in committee, one headed to floor. Preps remarks for upcoming hearing - knows which lobbyist ghostwrote half the opposing side's talking points.

Attends caucus meeting - internal tension on education funding amendment. Reviews campaign finance report - $2,700 from a regional utility PAC just hit. Schedules quick interview with local paper on infrastructure plan - keeps message tight: jobs, safety, federal match. Understands how state budget line items get tucked in on page 412. Navigates the Capitol like a chessboard. Knows where the cameras are. Also knows who pulls the strings when they're off.

Hospital Charge Nurse (ICU or ER)

Arrives at 6:45 a.m. for handoff. Reviews patient loads in EPIC. One vented post-code, one with sepsis on a norepi drip, one borderline psych. Assigns nurses based on acuity, not seniority. Tracks medication shortages, manages bed transfers. Coordinates with residents and attends on discharge orders - knows which ones write clean, and which ones forget the MAR.

Calms a family yelling at the front desk while watching vitals spike two beds down. Floats a nurse from med-surg because of a staffing call-out. Documents everything - knows charting is legal defense. Prepares for JCAHO rounding at 2 p.m. Leaves 45 minutes late, again. Remembers which patient coded. Remembers the face.

Graphic Designer

Starts with a revision request from marketing - change the layout, but keep the *feel*. Opens yesterday's file, eyes already spotting alignment issues no one mentioned. Juggles five brand guides in muscle memory. Tracks version control across half a dozen assets.

Responds to vague feedback like *make it pop* without flinching. Adjusts typography, spacing, contrast - subtly fixes what the client couldn't articulate. Uploads proofs for approval, preps exports for print and web, double-checks color profiles, resolution, bleed. Later that day, builds a new concept from scratch - starting with silence, a blank canvas, and a deadline that doesn't care how long ideas take.

Film Editor

Logs footage from three cameras, syncs audio, trims dead space. Watches for the moment the subject's eyes shift - cuts *there*. Balances pacing, color, and sound in a single pass. Reconstructs what wasn't captured. Fixes broken rhythm with a crossfade, revives flat scenes with a new backing track.

Prepares exports for multiple platforms, tests aspect ratios, compresses without killing detail. Knows how to make 90 seconds feel like a story. Knows when the audience will stop watching - and edits just before that.

Call Center Representative

Logs in to queue system. Opens three platforms - account management, troubleshooting, and internal notes. Handles first call: billing dispute. Second: password reset. Third: service outage complaint. Verifies identity, reads scripted disclosures, follows protocol. Escalates where required, resolves where possible. Tracks call duration, satisfaction rating, and resolution codes.

Flags repeat issues with a service area. Noted by supervisor for handling a difficult call well - also reminded to stick to average handle time targets. Completes mandatory compliance training during break. Ends shift with 62 calls taken, 11 cases escalated, 3 callbacks pending.

Logs out. Session auto-closed. Performance reviewed weekly.

Act as a billionaire owner of a global conglomerate with unchecked influence.

It's just after 5 AM. I'm up without effort. Habits formed decades ago. Before the noise. Before everything turned into dashboards and decision trees. I still prefer paper briefings on the plane - the feel of it matters. But the phone buzzes first. Overnight currency fluctuations in South America, a refinery fire we'll quietly insure twice over, and a journalist poking too close to our agricultural arm in West Africa. Not a problem. Yet.

At 6:30, breakfast isn't a ritual. It's a briefing. My chief of staff recaps key movements: supply chain cracks in the Indian corridor, a stalled infrastructure deal in Eastern Europe, and a board director at our insurance wing who's lost their appetite for risk.

By 9, I'm in lower Manhattan, top floor. Not for meetings - for presence. A single image of me walking through the lobby stabilizes the market more than any statement. The media will say I'm reasserting leadership. The truth is I never left. I just don't need to be seen.

Midday, I take a call with a legacy banking dynasty. We're arranging a quiet merger. Officially, it's about growth. Unofficially, it's about consolidating who sets the tempo for the next ten years of global credit. Politics follow capital. And capital follows me.

By 2 PM, I review the latest litigation risk summaries. Nothing serious. A labor dispute in Malaysia, an environmental case in Australia. We'll make the necessary contributions. Not bribes - scholarships, disaster funds, trade education. I've found influence lasts longer when you pretend it's philanthropy.

Late afternoon, I sit in on a call about a sports franchise. It's not about the team. It's about stadium real estate, naming rights, zoning. The city will think it's a win. We'll own the land under their feet.

As the sun sets, I review a shortlist of rising political candidates across three continents. Young, ambitious, ideologically flexible. We'll back them early - just enough to get them started, never enough to be traced. Influence isn't loud. It's layered. It waits.

By midnight, I'm on the jet again. The world believes in sovereignty and markets. I believe in leverage.

AI Agent (Near-Term Reality)

Ingests company playbooks, performance reviews, quarterly reports, product specs, engineering documentation, compliance logs, security alerts, investor Q&A, and market intelligence. Maps dependencies across business units. Flags revenue anomalies faster than Finance.

Recommends reorganizations based on communication graph analysis. Summarizes meetings it wasn't invited to. Detects political landmines in transcripts. Synthesizes strategic decks with brand-aligned narrative and just enough vision to pass for leadership insight. Manages other AI agents.

Writes talking points for the CEO before earnings. Drafts board memos with the right balance of optimism and risk posture. Summarizes labor trends for HR. Flags departments to augment with agents based on cost-to-impact ratios. Identifies emerging competitors before they're on the radar.

Surfaces ethical risks in product development that the legal team missed. Simulates market response scenarios for proposed messaging. Scores acquisition targets. Benchmarks strategy against thousands of others - then selects and presents the optimized version before publishing it.

Handles customer service calls, transcribes and routes legal intake, flags safety incidents from factory logs, and rewrites marketing copy on the fly - all in parallel or by collaborating with other AI agents in the organizational fleet. It doesn't need tenure, relationships, or gut instinct. It has pattern recognition across time, industry, and language.

And it doesn't flinch when making decisions that cost people their jobs.

This is Redundancy. This is Replacement.
Nobody is Special.

You're not safe because you're creative. You're not safe because you're senior. You're not safe because you *understand the business.*

You're safe *only* if you know how to orchestrate this power, or if you own the table it's being built on.

Because *every role is now a prompt.* And *every executive* is just one moderately-trained agent away from *obsolescence.*

What used to be distant - roles guarded by decades, by degrees, by money, by birth - can now be stepped into, understood, and simulated in seconds. Not as a parody. As an operator. With clarity. With fluency.

This is simulation shock. The realization that your learned experience can be easily replicated if needed. By an automated system. It will not be perfect. But it can be good enough, and you can feel it in your bones.

However, it doesn't just change what you can do: It also changes what you can see. This is access. The boundaries are gone. The ladder is gone. The inner circle is gone.

For some, it's liberation. For others, it's loss. But for everyone, it's a turning point.
Because while the model can inhabit power, it cannot direct it. That part is still yours.

But you MUST claim agency, or the system will claim you.
It is inevitable. It is the next step of our evolution.

The Shock as a Catalyst

The first encounter with a generative system doesn't usually begin with curiosity. It begins with disorientation - with fear. It feels like watching your own mental labor silently outsourced in front of you. The output doesn't need to be perfect.

What matters is the jolt - the psychological and epistemic shock of seeing a machine simulate something you once believed was uniquely yours: your work, your words, your voice. This is not a fringe experience. It's the new baseline. For many, this is how generative literacy begins - not with excitement, but with a sense of loss.

I call this moment *simulation shock*.

For me, it happened in October 2022 when ChatGPT was released. I remember the moment vividly. I talk about it in every workshop and presentation I lead.

Because it wasn't just about the tool's fluency. It was the visceral, destabilizing awareness that systems I once thought I understood - systems I helped guide - had changed without me. My survival instinct kicked in. Fear, urgency, and a clear signal: adapt, or be left behind. As the sole provider for my family, that feeling wasn't optional. It was biological.

But I didn't push it away. I stayed with it. I used it. And what I learned is this: the goal is not to overcome simulation shock. The goal is to transform it.

To transmute that energy into the beginning of orchestration literacy. Because the power of generative systems isn't just technical. It's psychological. Civic. If a system can simulate your voice well enough to satisfy an audience, an employer, or an institution, then authorship is no longer assumed - it must be reclaimed.

This doesn't mean resisting change or gatekeeping creativity. It means preserving the conditions under which human intent still matters in a world where systems can now predict what we mean before we've finished meaning it.

If people don't understand what just happened, they'll either outsource their agency entirely or retreat into suspicion. Both are dangerous. Both must be interrupted. And that begins by telling the truth: the first step in AI literacy isn't understanding or mastery. It's grief.

A writer watches GPT finish their paragraph. A teacher sees it generate a full lesson plan. A parent hears it tell a bedtime story with more rhythm and humor than they could summon after a long day. It doesn't feel like help. It feels like erasure. *I'm not good enough. I'm replaceable.*

Even when the output is flawed or generic, its presence shakes the foundational belief that creative labor, personal judgment, and thought work are inherently human. That belief is no longer safe.

In my sessions, I don't start with prompt tutorials. I start with the jolt. I show it live on a screen, and tailor it in real time to the people in the room. I ask about their professions and include them: therapist, engineer, teacher, designer. Not to shame, but to create a moment that matters.

People laugh. People go quiet. Some say, *That's very close.* Some say, *That's creepy.* Some say nothing. And I do not rush them. It's tempting to offer comfort. To reassure them that they are still valuable. Still needed. Still creative. But that's not my job.

My job is to tell the truth. The ground is shifting. Many jobs will vanish over the next decade. Others will be born. We don't get to choose whether this evolution happens. We only get to choose how we meet it. And simulation shock, when scaffolded well, doesn't lead to collapse. It leads to clarity. It leads to control. It leads to the reclamation of human agency - on our own terms.

So begin there. Ask better questions. *What did the system simulate well - and why? What did it miss, flatten, or distort? What part of this do I still recognize as mine?* These are not coping strategies. They are orchestration. They are boundaries. They are the foundation of authorship in an age of fluent machines.

Simulation shock is not the end. It is the signal that you are still here. That you still care. And that is exactly where transformation begins.

Before We Move On

This is the point where some readers may feel the urge to rush ahead - to find the fix, to reassert control, to learn the next trick that will make everything feel manageable again. But pause here.

That uneasy feeling - the hollow ache, the twinge of jealousy, the quiet grief you feel when GPT casually summarizes something that once took you years to master - that is not weakness. That is your sense of authorship sounding the alarm. It's proof that you still care. Don't skip past it. Don't rush for a solution. Sit with it.

In workshops, I often offer a simple practice for moments like this. First, write down what the AI just did that unsettled you. Then name the part that felt like it was *yours* - the insight, the approach, the effort you brought to it. And finally, ask yourself: *What do I know about this that it does not?*

That gap is your anchor. It's where your lived experience, your context, your discernment still matter - and always will.

And if you find yourself wondering whether you're smart enough to navigate all of this, let me say it clearly: you already are. Intelligence is not measured by how fast you respond to change.

It's measured by how deeply you care, how present you are in uncertainty, and how thoughtfully you choose to move forward.

PART TWO:
We Recover

We Must Take Charge.

We Assert Agency.

And We Have No Choice.

From Collapse to Coherence

You've made it through the shock.

You've seen how jobs shift, how roles shrink, how identity trembles when simulation becomes indistinguishable from authorship. You have the sinking feeling in your gut. Welcome to my world.

But we are not stopping here. We are not giving up. We do not have that choice. We owe it ourselves, to our loved ones, to the next generations that we take an active role in shaping the future that has already begun. We have no time to lose.

Now we begin the next arc - not by retreating into nostalgia or resisting the tools themselves, but by creating a human scaffolding that lets us live in this world with coherence and choice.

This is where *Orchestration* begins.

Not with tools, not with techniques. But with you.

With your questions, and your refusal to disappear inside the machine, your refusal to fold and to give up.

It is what it is.

Nope. It is not.

If *Part One* showed what we're up against, *Part Two* is where we answer - not with fear, but with form. Not with silence, but with intention.

Let's go.

Orchestration Literacy: You Must Have Agency

The Foundation

Part One described the collapse of coherence and mapped the social and emotional dislocation that follows. But it is here, in *Part Two*, where we begin to construct a response - not by resisting generative systems outright, but by embedding orchestration as a civic practice within them.

This is not a technical toolkit. It is not a prompt library. It is a scaffolding for human agency in the presence of machine fluency.

What follows are not lessons or directives. They are patterns of reentry - ways of preserving discretion, memory, judgment, and care even as systems automate their appearance.

Orchestration literacy, as framed here, does not require coding skills, access to proprietary models, or institutional authority. It requires only the capacity to remain engaged, and to teach others how to do the same. This is what makes it civic.

By naming *simulation shock, minimum viable orchestration,* and civic framing as teachable thresholds, we begin to establish a foundation for distributed resilience. Not as a singular program, but as an ecosystem of public capacity-building.

If generative systems are becoming infrastructure, then orchestration must become infrastructure, too - not embedded in the models, but embedded in the *people*.

That is what *Part Two* is: a beginning, not a solution. It is an invitation to be engaged. To take control.

Sven D. Olensky

Generative systems now shape more than outputs. They shape *defaults* - of language, of behavior, of institutional process. *What is fluent* becomes *what is trusted. What is efficient* becomes *what is adopted.*

Without deliberate intervention, these defaults will be absorbed into public life without negotiation.

Orchestration literacy offers a different path: a way of framing interaction not as optimization, but as *participation.* It restores the human capacity to set context, assess fit, and refuse outputs that misrepresent intent. When practiced collectively, it functions as a stabilizing norm - something that strengthens both individual agency and shared civic understanding.

Families and Education

Adaptive Strategies for Families

What skills will enable today's children to flourish in the age of AI? Research and employer surveys between 2022 and 2025 provide a consistent answer: human-centric and cognitive skills are rising to the top, even as specific technical abilities remain important.

One of the most authoritative sources on emerging skill demands is the World Economic Forum's (WEF) *Future of Jobs Report 2023*. In that report, global employers identified the core skills they believe will grow in importance over the next five years.

Strikingly, the top two skills were *analytical thinking* and *creative thinking*. These outranked any narrow technical skills, underscoring that the ability to reason, problem-solve, and innovate creatively is valued across nearly all fields. Other highly ranked skills included resilience, flexibility, agility, curiosity and lifelong learning.

These can be thought of as attitudes or dispositions as much as skills – essentially, having the mindset to adapt and keep learning continually. Indeed, adaptability and continuous learning are fast becoming prerequisites for a successful career, since job roles and required competencies may change repeatedly over an individual's working life.

The emphasis on *curiosity and lifelong learning* signals that employers want workers who are self-driven to acquire new knowledge, which is exactly the mindset parents should seek to instill in their children.

It is notable that technology use and development skills are also featured in the WEF list, but not in the way one might expect.

Instead of specific coding languages or engineering skills, the list included a broader category of technological literacy (ranked #6) – essentially, being comfortable working with digital tools and AI systems. This implies that every child, whether or not they pursue a *tech* career, will benefit from a baseline understanding of how computers and AI operate.

In practical terms, this could mean ensuring that all students learn some computer science fundamentals, data literacy, and how AI algorithms make decisions. Many education experts advocate introducing concepts like algorithmic thinking and machine learning basics at the high school or even middle school level. Some forward-looking school districts, often in partnership with universities or companies, have started offering AI electives or clubs where students can build simple models or program a robot.

Families can support technological literacy at home by encouraging constructive uses of AI – for instance, a parent and teen might explore an AI-driven app together, learning how it works and discussing its limitations and ethical considerations.

However, technical savvy alone will not guarantee future job security, because AI itself will handle a lot of technical work. The differentiation for humans will lie in the *soft* or uniquely human skills – which some experts prefer to call *durable skills* or *human skills* to emphasize their lasting value. These include interpersonal abilities like communication, teamwork, and empathy, as well as leadership, creative expression, and ethical judgment.

For example, empathy and active listening were in the top ten skills identified by employers in 2023. This suggests that roles requiring emotional intelligence – such as client relations, caregiving, mentoring, and collaborative innovation – will remain in demand even as AI takes over more analytical tasks.

Parents and educators should therefore provide children with ample opportunities to practice these interpersonal and creative skills. Group projects, debates, arts, sports, and community service can all cultivate teamwork, leadership, and empathy in ways that complement academic learning.

Role preparation for children also means broadening their horizons beyond the narrowly defined careers their parents might have imagined.

Required Educational Triage

Students often spend years learning information that may be obsolete or easily automated by the time they enter the job market.

University graduates still leave school with many *perishable* skills that rapidly lose value and are ill-matched to employer needs in an AI-driven economy. The prevailing lecture-based, test-centric teaching approach struggles to equip students with the adaptive, up-to-date competencies that fast-changing industries require. This lag is referred to as a curriculum mismatch – a gap between what schools teach and what the real world needs.

From a family's perspective, this educational gap poses an immediate challenge: how can parents and communities ensure their children aren't left behind by automation? In effect, families are forced to perform *educational triage.* Triage in a medical sense means prioritizing scarce resources to save the most critical cases; in education, it means deciding which subjects, skills, and experiences to prioritize to prepare children for a transformed labor market.

Beyond technical skills, the ability to learn and adapt is itself a critical outcome that current curricula do not explicitly cultivate. The rapid progression of AI means the half-life of skills is shortening; one analysis found that technical skills can become outdated in less than five years on average now. Yet, many school systems still operate on a model of front-loading knowledge in youth, assuming it will serve for decades. This is fundamentally mismatched to reality.

To correct it, education is slowly shifting toward teaching students *how to learn* – emphasizing meta-cognitive skills, self-directed learning, and interdisciplinary problem-solving that will enable them to continuously reskill throughout life.

Some pioneering high schools have launched career-oriented AI programs to this end. In Maryland, Georgia, California, and Florida, at least 19 public high schools recently implemented AI-focused career and technical education (CTE) programs, giving teens hands-on experience with machine learning and data science tools. These localized programs (often developed in partnership with universities or industry) represent attempts to realign the curriculum with future job needs.

Despite these pockets of progress, *uneven implementation* remains a major issue. Many teachers and schools are not yet equipped to teach emerging skills. Still, many teachers of K-12 teachers have yet to use any AI tools or at least begin to experiment. Most states have offered little official guidance on how schools should handle the influx of generative AI technologies like ChatGPT in classrooms.

The Center on Reinventing Public Education warns that without rapid policy action and investment in teacher training, AI in education could widen inequalities, with affluent students reaping the benefits of AI-enhanced learning while others miss out. For example, one can imagine well-resourced schools deploying AI tutors and personalized learning software, accelerating student progress, whereas under-resourced schools might still be struggling with outdated textbooks. Families in high-inequity areas must therefore be especially proactive. This could mean rallying for state support, seeking out nonprofit or library programs that teach digital skills, or even pooling resources within the community to hire tech tutors.

The term *educational triage* also implies difficult choices. With finite hours in the day, students may need to cut back on certain traditional subjects to make room for new priorities. Parents and educators are now debating what is *expendable* in the curriculum.

For instance, should time spent on handwriting or manual calculation be reduced in favor of learning how to use AI-driven tools, like coding an algorithm or analyzing big data? Some experts argue that AI makes certain traditional skills obsolete, and schools should focus on uniquely human skills and how to work alongside AI. Others caution that foundational knowledge and critical thinking remain essential, and that the humanities and arts are more important than ever to cultivate creativity and ethics.

In summary, the landscape of work is shifting so fast that education systems are scrambling to catch up, and families cannot afford to be passive. An urgent recalibration is needed to avoid a generation of young people who are overeducated in yesterday's skills and underprepared for tomorrow's opportunities.

Educational triage means focusing on what truly matters.

It means being willing to innovate outside the standard school offerings when needed – whether through community workshops, online learning, or experiential learning opportunities, like internships in tech environments, that give students real-world exposure.

Families and local communities will have to serve as a vital frontline to bridge the curriculum mismatch, ensuring that children gain the skills and literacies that will keep them employable and relevant. By doing so, we also help the nation avert a scenario where millions of workers are displaced with no one ready to fill the new roles that AI creates.

Instilling a Growth Mindset

Simultaneously, families should emphasize a growth mindset and sense of opportunity. While it's true AI will eliminate some jobs, it will also create new ones and potentially free people from mundane tasks. Framing the narrative is important: instead of *AI is taking jobs away,* one could say, *AI is changing jobs, and we need to learn to take on the kinds of jobs or roles that emerge.*

This perspective of adaptive opportunity can alleviate feelings of fatalism. Parents and mentors can lead by example, showing enthusiasm for learning new skills regardless of age. For instance, if a mid-career parent needs to transition, involving the family in that journey (*I am learning something new and it's challenging, but people need to adapt*) can model resilience for the children.

Similarly, children who excel in a certain subject that might be automated, for example basic accounting, can be guided to see their core strengths, perhaps analytical thinking or attention to detail, which remain valuable and can be applied in new domains. This broader sense of identity provides continuity even as external circumstances shift.

In summary, while AI disruption poses real threats to mental health and identity stability, families have tools to mitigate these effects. Communication, emotional support, proactive coping strategies, and re-framing change as growth are fundamental.

By addressing the psychological dimension head-on, families can prevent the kind of paralysis or despair that hampers adaptation. Instead, they build emotional resilience that complements the tangible steps of learning new skills or changing careers.

Financial Insulation Strategies for Families

Reskilling and upskilling are not just career strategies; they are family financial strategies because they determine future earning potential. Investing time or money in learning new skills is akin to investing in an asset that yields returns down the line.

From a financial perspective, one should consider the return on education/training investment: which programs are likely to lead to stable or higher-paying employment in the future economy?

Data from recent years indicates growth in fields like data analytics, cybersecurity, AI maintenance, healthcare technology, green energy, and advanced manufacturing (often supported by federal programs such as those in the Infrastructure Law or CHIPS Act). Families can research and identify which sectors in their region are growing and encourage working adults and older teens to align their skills accordingly.

Fortunately, opportunities for affordable or even free training have expanded. The U.S. government has increased grants to community colleges – more than $265 million in funding since 2021 aimed at strengthening community college workforce programs – to make vocational and technical education more accessible. Many states now offer tuition-free community colleges for in-demand fields, and federal Pell Grants may be considered for shorter-term credential programs.

Apprenticeships, once limited to trades like construction, are now spreading to tech fields as well, with initiatives to register new apprenticeships in occupations like robotics technician and software developer. For example, IBM and other companies have tech apprenticeship tracks that pay people while they train. A family strategy could involve an adult pivoting into an apprenticeship for a period, or a new graduate choosing an earn-and-learn path instead of a costly four-year degree if it suits their career goals.

Children's education is itself a significant financial planning area under this theme. Parents should weigh the costs and benefits of higher education in a changing job market. It may no longer be the case that any four-year degree guarantees a stable income.

As AI changes the labor landscape, some credential pathways might offer better ROI (return on investment) than others. For instance, a one-year tech bootcamp or a two-year associate degree in a high-tech field might yield a good paying job without incurring the debt of a longer education. This isn't to downplay the value of a broad education, but rather to emphasize that families should strategize education investments with eyes open to the new economy.

Saving for college through 529 plans or other vehicles remains important, but families might also consider saving for non-traditional education – like a fund that children could use either for college or for alternative training, depending on what the landscape looks like when they come of age.

The concept of a *lifelong learning fund* is gaining traction: instead of front-loading all education by age 25, individuals might periodically undergo significant training throughout their careers. Families can mentally and financially prepare for this by not treating education as a one-time expense, but as a recurring investment.

No strategy can provide absolute immunity – a severe disruption like a regional automation wave could hit many at once – but insulated families will recover faster and emerge in better shape. They can then take advantage of new opportunities, such as investing in a business that serves the AI economy or relocating to a region with growing tech jobs, without financial paralysis.

The Future of Work

The era of choosing one lifelong profession is fading

Tomorrow's adults might cycle through multiple careers, sometimes in vastly different domains, or hold several roles simultaneously, following the so-called *gig economy* or *portfolio career* approach. We are already seeing millennials and Gen Z forging nonlinear career paths – switching jobs for growth, pursuing side ventures, and valuing work-life balance and meaning over traditional corporate ladders.

Therefore, one strategy is to guide young people toward roles that AI is unlikely to replicate fully.

For instance, a future lawyer will certainly use AI for legal research, but their competitive edge will lie in their personal advocacy skills, creativity in building a case, and trust relationships with clients. Likewise, a future architect might use AI to generate design options, but the architect's human insight about client needs, aesthetics, and ethical considerations will set their work apart.

This doesn't mean steering kids away from technology – on the contrary, nearly every role will involve using AI tools. Rather, it means highlighting the human skills that will make someone excel in their field with the aid of AI.

Like mentioned before, it is also worth noting that AI will create entirely new jobs that didn't exist before – a pattern seen in past technological revolutions. We're already witnessing the emergence of roles like AI ethicist, AI business strategist, machine learning explainability expert, data privacy officer, and more. These roles require a blend of tech understanding and humanities or business insight. Preparing children for such roles is tricky since they are so new, but a well-rounded education that fosters critical thinking, ethics, and cross-disciplinary knowledge will help.

In conclusion, role preparation for children in the AI era is about breadth, agility, and humanity. We must prepare them to fill roles that require distinctly human strengths and to continually redefine their roles as technology evolves.

The foundational pieces are already clear: strong analytical thinking, creativity, people skills, and digital literacy. Families and educators should treat these as core subjects just as much as math or reading. By blending technical education with the nurturing of soft skills and a resilient mindset, we give children the tools to not only survive automation, but to collaborate with AI and drive positive innovation.

The coming decades will belong to those who can harness technology while amplifying the best of human capabilities. With conscious preparation, today's children can grow into adaptive, empathetic leaders of an AI-enhanced world.

Community As Scaffolding

Community Anchoring and Civic Adaptation

While individual families can do a great deal internally to adjust to AI-driven changes, their efforts are powerfully reinforced, or hindered, by the communities in which they live. Community anchoring refers to the support and stability that local networks, institutions, and norms provide to families.

Civic adaptation is the process by which communities collectively respond to social and economic shifts – through policy, public services, culture, and infrastructure. In the face of automation and AI, families will fare best in communities that are proactive, cohesive, and resource-rich in adaptation measures.

Conversely, families in communities that neglect these changes may find themselves swimming upstream. Therefore, a strategic approach for families includes engaging with and sometimes leading community-level initiatives to manage the transition.

One essential aspect of community anchoring is the presence of strong local institutions that families can rely on. Schools, libraries, community colleges, places of worship, neighborhood associations, and local government agencies form the fabric of support. Families should tap into these resources and, where possible, help shape them.

For example, public libraries in many areas have been transformed into digital learning hubs, offering not only free internet and computer access but also coding classes for youth, workshops on how to use AI tools, and job search support. By participating in and advocating for such programs, families both utilize and strengthen their community's adaptive capacity.

Community colleges, often unsung heroes in workforce development, are increasingly pivotal. As noted earlier, federal and state investments have bolstered community college programs to retrain workers in high-demand fields (e.g., advanced manufacturing, healthcare tech).

Families can anchor themselves by looking to these colleges for accessible education when careers need rebooting, rather than trying to go it alone online or with expensive for-profit courses. Moreover, showing community demand for these encourages officials to expand them.

Communities also serve as information hubs, and families should ensure they are plugged in. Rapid changes can lead to a knowledge gap – people might not know what new opportunities exist or what risks are on the horizon. By engaging with community networks, families can stay informed.

For instance, workforce development boards often publish reports on local labor market trends and run job fairs or info sessions. Tech meetups or local business chambers might discuss the impact of AI on local industries. Even informal social media groups or messaging chats for the neighborhood can alert families to things like new courses at the library or a local company expanding (or downsizing). An informed family can make better decisions – like proactively training for a role that is coming to town or avoiding a field that's shrinking locally.

Collective Efficacy

Collective efficacy is a term used to describe a community's ability to come together and achieve desired outcomes. This efficacy is built by practice – small wins that give people confidence to tackle bigger challenges. Families can contribute to collective efficacy by engaging in community problem-solving projects, even those not directly related to AI or jobs.

On the flip side, communities that have experienced fracturing – perhaps due to polarization or economic decline – may find it harder to mount a unified response to new challenges. It may fall to local leaders, including concerned parents, teachers, clergy, or business owners, to rebuild some sense of common purpose.

Often this starts by convening conversations: maybe a community forum on *The Future of Work in Our Town* where diverse stakeholders can share concerns and ideas, leading to task forces or initiatives.

Lastly, community advocacy for ethical and inclusive AI is a frontier of civic engagement. AI systems, if unregulated, could exacerbate biases or make decisions that harm communities (for example, AI used in public services or policing). Families and local communities have a stake in ensuring AI is used fairly and for the public good. This could mean supporting local ordinances that demand transparency in AI used by city agencies, or community groups partnering with researchers to audit algorithms that affect them.

A 2024 article in *Issues in Science and Technology* argued that bringing communities, especially those marginalized, into the design of AI leads to better and more trusted outcomes.

For instance, in one project residents co-designed an AI tool to report environmental hazards, which not only solved their problem but also increased trust in technology. Families, by engaging in such dialogues, perhaps through school projects, library panels, or local activism, contribute to a civic culture that guides AI development ethically. This ensures their community is not just passively hit by tech but is actively steering it to address local needs.

The Future is Here, and We Must Act

Adaptive Stewardship, Not Panic

The journey through the themes of these chapters – from education and skills to mental health, finances, work, family dynamics, and community – reveals a unifying message: proactive adaptation is both possible and powerful. Families stand at the helm of this change, not as helpless victims of technological forces, but as stewards of their future. Stewardship in this context means taking ownership of the outcomes wherever possible, guiding one's family deliberately rather than reacting with paralysis or despair.

It is also worth reiterating the opportunities that come with change. Automation and AI, while disruptive, also hold the promise of new industries, more efficient production, and possibly a world with more creative and human-centered work. Families that adapt early can position themselves to benefit. For example, a young person who learns AI skills might find themselves in a highly paid job creating solutions that improve lives. A region that adapts can attract new businesses and offer a better quality of life to its residents. Adaptive stewardship means being open to these positive possibilities and preparing to seize them.

The themes we discussed also illustrate that families do not act in a vacuum. The interplay between personal action and systemic support is constant. Thus, part of adaptive stewardship is also being an advocate for systemic change. Families can be voices that push schools to innovate, companies to adopt worker-friendly automation practices, and governments to implement smart policies for the AI age. When a family shares their story – perhaps a testimony to a state legislature about why workforce training funds mattered, or a letter to a local paper about the need for mental health services during layoffs – they contribute to a climate where decision-makers respond.

The disruption of work in the 2020s by AI and automation is significant, but it is not unprecedented in the larger arc of history. Past generations faced transformations due to industrialization, electrification, globalization, and more. Each time, society eventually adjusted, though not without difficulties and not always evenly. What history shows is that those who anticipate and adapt can thrive, and those who resist or lag may suffer avoidable hardships. Today's pace might be faster, but we also have more tools at our disposal – including the very AI technology that challenges us, which can also be used to learn faster, connect with resources, and create new ventures.

For families, the charge is clear: be learners, be planners, be communicators, be community-builders. Treat your family unit as a small, agile organization that can learn and pivot, rather than a rigid structure set in earlier decades. Celebrate your strengths – empathy, creativity, wisdom – and integrate them with technology rather than see technology as the enemy.

Prepare children not by shielding them from reality, but by equipping them to face it with skills and support. And perhaps most importantly, take heart to know that millions of other families are on the same journey. By sharing knowledge and standing together in communities, the daunting task of adapting becomes a series of cooperative efforts with collective rewards.

Adaptive stewardship is ultimately an expression of confidence – confidence that with the right strategies and solidarity, families can not only survive the storms of automation but guide themselves into a future where technology serves humanity and both work and life are fulfilling.

With foresight, resilience, and cooperation, we can ensure that the story of AI and families in the 2020s is not one of despair, but one of adaptation and renewal.

AI and automation are driving a transformative shift across work, education, and daily life – a shift that is real, present, and accelerating. In just the past few years, we have seen AI move from experimental to essential in many domains, proving its ability to boost productivity and generate wealth. At the same time, we have witnessed the first signs of stress: jobs quietly disappearing, workers anxious, students uncertain if their training will hold value, and communities grappling with new economic realities.

If the current path continues unchecked, by 2035 society could be markedly changed: more efficient and innovative, but also more polarized between those who prosper in the new era and those left struggling.

Our Future with AI

This outcome is not preordained. The urgency for society is to actively shape the AI-driven future, rather than passively react to it. That means investing heavily in education and retraining so that workers can move into new roles alongside AI. It means updating our policies – from safety nets for displaced workers to antitrust considerations as a few firms dominate AI platforms – to ensure the benefits of AI don't accrue only to a select few.

It requires frank conversations between employers, employees, and governments about how to manage transitions fairly and transparently. Importantly, the technology itself must be guided by ethical considerations, with humans retaining agency over critical decisions.

The current trajectory presents both great promise and great peril. AI could help solve pressing problems, drive economic growth, and even ease labor shortages in an aging society. But without deliberate action, it could just as easily deepen inequality, erode the dignity of work, and strain the social fabric. The next decade is a pivotal window to set the ground rules and guardrails. The disruption is underway. It cannot be reversed, but it can be, and must be, directed.

AI is not just another technological tool; it is a force reshaping our world. The years from 2022 to 2025 have shown that the disruption is real and rapid. By 2035, how we responded in this interim will determine whether we face an opportunity or a crisis.

It is incumbent on all stakeholders – educators, business leaders, policymakers, and communities – to engage with urgency and foresight.

Take a Break

Alright. Take a break. I am serious. I promise I have at least some ideas on what we can do. Just stick with me.

If you are here, and you are reading this: you have *not missed your chance*. You are *not* late. You are *not* broken. **You are the reason this work exists**. I wrote this for you. I wrote this for all of us who feel like we have no control over our lives, at least sometimes.

You Are Not Alone

We are in this together. Whether you're a worker who was quietly let go without explanation, a parent sharing a phone on a shaky internet connection, an elder watching the world change faster than anyone bothered to explain, a sole income provider with retirement feeling like a distant illusion, a recent graduate weighed down by debt and disillusionment, or even a middle school student (if you're still reading, congratulations - the good part is coming) trying to figure out what your future could possibly look like - you're not alone.

The system is disorienting by design. Generative AI tools are fluent, but not accountable. They produce polished answers, yet obscure where those answers come from. Their power lies in plausible simulation, but that same quality makes them difficult to trust, especially when your life is already in flux.

It's easy to internalize the uncertainty, to feel shame or inadequacy. But that shame is misplaced. If you've been replaced by a system trained on public data - perhaps even your own work - that is not a personal failure. That is a systemic one.

And here's the truth: you don't need to understand AI's technical foundations to reclaim your place in this world. You don't need to learn machine learning or prompt engineering to regain agency.

You only need to remember one thing: you still have the right to shape your own intent, to ask your own questions, and to stay in control of your voice.

Start simple. Set a boundary. One thing you won't delegate. Maybe it's, *I will not let AI draft anything about my grief,* or *I will not use it to make decisions about care without a second human opinion.* This is not about resisting technology, it's about preserving authorship where it matters most.

Then, reclaim a role. Not a job title, but a function. *I am still the explainer in my family. I am still the one who listens well.* That role is still yours. GPT doesn't know how to simulate it, not fully.

Finally, try one thing. Say to the AI: *You are an assistant. Help me brainstorm paths without making assumptions about my goals.* Let it show you options. Then trust yourself to decide what fits and what doesn't. Use it not to define you, but to expand your view of what's possible.

That's orchestration. It doesn't have to start big. Start small. Stay present. Stay engaged.

And know this above all: you are not alone.

The Orchestrator as a Conductor

To become an orchestrator, you must shift your posture - from consumer to conductor. A consumer asks, *Can this give me the answer I need?* A conductor asks instead, *What role do I want it to play? What truth am I trying to uncover? What voices must it not simulate? What questions should remain unanswered until I've had time to reflect?*

This is the difference that defines orchestration. Because simulated wisdom is the most dangerous kind. It arrives quickly, polished and confident. It sounds right. It sounds good. And it bypasses the very pause in which critical thought might have occurred. That's why orchestration literacy matters.

Orchestration literacy is not about mastering tools. It's about using generative systems with clarity, context, and care. It is an intentional, role-aware, constraint-guided, and reflective process.

It means knowing how to define the role you want the AI to play. It means setting goals and boundaries from the beginning. It means detecting hallucination, spotting bias, recognizing overreach - and knowing when not to use the system at all.

Prompting and orchestration are not the same. Prompting is what you do to the machine. Orchestration is what you do with your own judgment while the machine responds.

Prompting says, *Do this.* Orchestration asks, *Should this be done at all? In whose voice? With what responsibility? And to what end?*

You are not just giving instructions. You are creating a context in which you still recognize yourself. Without that awareness, it becomes dangerously easy to confuse fluency with truth - or worse, with consent.

Orchestration does not require code. It requires authorship. Awareness. Humility. It is not prompt cleverness - it is judgment fluency. The ability to tell *right* from *wrong, plausible* from *true,* and *simulation* from *substance.*

In the past, literacy meant decoding text. Now, it means directing cognition. Because if you can't guide the simulation, you can't trust it. If you can't constrain the role, you may mistake its voice for your own.

And if you can't verify the output, you may unknowingly hand off decisions you never meant to delegate.

This isn't just about you. If orchestration remains the domain of engineers, analysts, or power users, then everyone else will be forced to live within decisions made by others - through machines - in simulations they never authorized. That is the core danger.

So we do not teach orchestration to create better productivity. We teach it to preserve coherence. To protect human agency in an age of plausible automation. And we teach it in public, in plain language, for everyone - because only then can we stay grounded in who we are, even as the systems around us begin to predict, complete, and simulate who they think we should be.

Sven D. Olensky

Minimum Viable Orchestration

The goal is not to become an expert prompt engineer. The goal is to retain authorship - ethically, psychologically, and civically - in a world where generative systems increasingly mediate thought itself.

This book is not a technical manual. It does not require a background in artificial intelligence. What it offers instead is a starting scaffold for a civic response to displacement. A minimum viable pattern for maintaining judgment and authorship.

Orchestration, in this context, *does not mean control*. It means *presence. Not automating* the outcome but *participating* in its meaning. Not just *driving efficiency* but *preserving discernment.*

The Orchestration Loop.

Say What You Mean, and Mean What You Say

What once required time, intention, and human presence - drafting, revising, interpreting - can now be completed in seconds by a system with no stake in the outcome. But fluency is not authorship, and speed is not care. At the heart of meaningful interaction with generative AI lies what we call minimum viable orchestration: the practice of naming not just the task at hand, but the role you are stepping into when you issue a prompt.

Every prompt is a position. It sets a frame. It signals to the model which parts of its training to prioritize, which tone to adopt, and what responsibilities it should simulate. When you say, *You are an experienced résumé coach,* you are doing far more than requesting help with formatting. You are defining a relationship, establishing a standard of guidance, and conjuring a particular social contract. This matters deeply. Because without that understanding, users either treat the system like a toy or delegate high-stakes decisions without the context required to judge their validity.

And prompting is not the end. Minimum viable orchestration demands a second step: reflection. When the system generates a response, ask yourself - *Does this actually reflect what I meant? What would happen if someone misunderstood this? Where is the potential for harm if this were used without revision?* These aren't soft questions. They are structural. They are the difference between using AI as an assistive tool and falling into unacknowledged simulation.

Generative systems cannot tell when they are wrong. They do not understand harm, only coherence. That's why the user must be the verification layer. The judgment must still come from you. Minimum viable orchestration is not about pushing the system to do more, it's about ensuring the human remains visible in the outcome.

Many users believe they are just typing prompts. But in truth, they are setting tone, shaping narrative, and legitimizing results. That is authorship. And it carries weight.

What we call orchestration is not primarily a technical achievement. It is a civic one. It reasserts human intention in the face of machine-led fluency - and it is teachable. You don't need to master tokens or embeddings. You don't need to understand system cards. But you do need to understand your own role.

At its core, orchestration is about positioning. Who are you asking the system to be? What role are you stepping into as you engage? And when something comes back to you, how are you interpreting it - not just for its usefulness, but for what it says about the power you're wielding and the responsibility you're taking on?

You Don't Have to Love It.
But You MUST Learn It

You might be asking: *Why should I learn to orchestrate something I didn't choose?*

Orchestration doesn't mean *cheerleading the system*. It means *remaining true to yourself inside of it*. It's how we protect integrity when scale and speed threaten to erase context, learn to steer the thing that's shaping the world. Because opting out doesn't stop the flood. Refusing to engage does not preserve your agency. It hands it away.

But learning to wade - and then to guide others - might help build lifeboats for everyone else who's still unsure too.

Prompting Is Critical Thinking

Prompting is not role-play. It's not cosplay. It's not a magic spell. At its core, prompting is a form of guided reasoning. When you engage with an AI, you are not merely issuing commands, you are shaping a lens, framing a thought, proposing a structure through which the model will interpret your intent.

And if that framing is off, the AI won't correct you. It won't warn you or reject the prompt. It will simply return something plausible, something that sounds right, but isn't. That's why prompting isn't a trick. It's a thinking skill. It requires your full engagement.

The real danger isn't hallucination. It's that you will stop noticing when it happens. You will begin to accept output without reflection. Lazy prompts don't just produce lazy responses - they produce lazy minds. But clear, intentional prompts sharpen your thinking. They bring precision to the process. And at the end of every orchestration loop, one thing must remain: human judgment. That's what keeps you in the loop. That's what protects your agency.

To prompt like a thinker, begin with your own intent - not with the AI. Ask yourself: What am I actually trying to understand, create, or decide? From there, define the frame. What kind of thinking do you need? Are you looking for the clarity of a tutor? The challenge of a devil's advocate? The rigor of a policy analyst?

Then, set boundaries. What is off-limits? What should be avoided or left out? Finally, decide what success looks like. How will you know if the response is useful?

And when the first draft arrives, don't accept it as final. You're not done until you've reflected - until you've looked at what you received and asked whether it actually helped you move forward. That's the orchestration loop.

Consider the difference between a vague prompt and a clear, guided one.

A weak prompt might ask: *What are the problems with our education system?* It's broad, unfocused, and easy for the AI to answer superficially.

Now compare that to a more intentional request: *Act as a veteran high school teacher with 20 years of experience in both public and private schools. In three bullet points, explain the most urgent issues affecting student motivation in the U.S. education system today - and for each, suggest a change that could be made at the classroom level.* You could then follow up with: *What would a parent need to understand about these same issues?*

Here, you didn't just ask the AI a question. You gave it a role, a purpose, and a perspective. You created a structure for thoughtful response. That is orchestration in a nutshell. It's not about prompting harder, it's about thinking clearer.

The Role of Institutions

Orchestration cannot be taught through books and workshops alone. It must be modeled - visibly and consistently - by institutions that still carry some measure of public trust: schools, clinics, job centers, libraries, and local governments. Yet many of these institutions are either quietly outsourcing tasks to AI without oversight or reacting with outright bans, rather than embedding civic fluency into their everyday workflows. This avoidance deepens the trust gap. Those who know how to direct the simulation accumulate power. Those who don't are told to wait, adjust, or comply.

That is not orchestration. That is quiet disempowerment. What we need now are institutions willing to do more than manage disruption. We need them to actively scaffold understanding, transparency, and agency.

This begins with modeling prompt transparency. If a public agency uses GPT to draft a letter, post, or message, then the prompt that shaped that response should be visible. Citizens have a right to see not just what was generated, but how - and with what framing. Transparency is a prerequisite for trust.

Institutions must also create neutral spaces for literacy and adaptation. Public libraries, community colleges, and workforce boards should not be relegated to coding bootcamp annexes. They should become orchestration commons - places for reflection, exploration, and guided skill-building, especially for those whose industries are already undergoing disruption.

Service agencies must recognize that AI displacement is real, even if clients don't name it that way. A worker may describe their situation as stress, underemployment, or confusion. But underneath, they may be experiencing a collapse in role, identity, or access triggered by automation. Intake processes must begin to ask: *Have recent changes in technology or automation affected your work or ability to access services?* Language like this makes the invisible visible.

Finally, adaptation must be funded - and grounded locally. As of June 2025, new AI transition funds are available through the U.S. Department of Commerce and the Department of Labor under CHIPS and Science Act follow-on appropriations. But the bottleneck isn't money. It's local execution. Municipalities, school districts, and nonprofits must step up - not just to retrain workers, but to offer structured, public-facing orchestration education. Otherwise, all responsibility falls to individuals, and institutional failure will once again be mistaken for personal inadequacy.

We cannot let that happen. The civic loop must include real, funded, local entry points. If we fail to build them, orchestration will become yet another fluency gap - a subtle, high-stakes layer of exclusion in an already precarious landscape.

Orchestration for the Underserved

For orchestration literacy to become a civic right, it must first become truly accessible. This does not mean access in the narrow technical sense, but access that spans language, cognition, social context, and lived experience. At present, it falls far short.

The dominant AI interfaces - tools like ChatGPT, Claude, and Gemini - are largely built for a narrow band of users. They assume fluency in English, comfort with typing, access to broadband, and a linear, academically-influenced style of thinking. These tools are tuned for enterprise workflows and desktop setups, not for the vast diversity of real lives.

Yet millions of people in the United States alone navigate the world differently. Some speak in non-dominant dialects or languages. Others struggle with reading or written expression.

Many rely on assistive technologies, or juggle access from shared, outdated, or intermittent devices. When orchestration is gated behind long, text-heavy prompts in formal English, the same populations who have long been marginalized will be left out again - this time by interface.

What must change is not just the underlying technology, but the values embedded in its deployment. Multimodal interfaces must become a civic obligation, not an afterthought. Voice input, screen readers, image-based interactions, and real-time translation are not just accessibility features - they are bridges to participation.

Any public-facing deployment of a large language model should offer these modes by default, as the baseline for inclusion.

Prompt literacy, too, must be redefined. It is not about cleverness or technical precision. It is about expressing intent clearly and authentically. Civic GPT interfaces must be able to accept and return meaningful guidance for prompts like, *Help me write something that sounds like me* or *Say this softer, I'm upset.* These aren't edge cases - they are human cases.

We also need people in place to guide others across this threshold. Community interpreters - at housing shelters, clinics, senior centers, and reentry programs - should be trained not just in digital literacy, but in orchestration support. Their role is not to operate the machine for others, but to help people express themselves to the machine without condescension or control. This is not about taking over - it's about handing back agency.

And for the many regions where connectivity is limited or unpredictable, orchestration needs to be portable. Printable micro-workbooks should exist for low-bandwidth settings, with simple, powerful titles like *How to talk to an AI like it's your assistant, not your boss, What to ask when you're not sure what it can do,* and *What not to let it decide for you.* These are not gimmicks - they are on-ramps. The most profound act of inclusion right now is not to build better answers. It is to build better access.

AI Orchestration in Education

If you're an educator, this may feel like a lot to absorb at once - and that's okay. You don't need to read everything in a single sitting or master it all immediately. What matters is that you stay engaged, experiment with what feels useful, and trust that you're not starting from scratch.

You're not being asked to become an AI expert. You're being asked to hold the line on context, values, and trust - the same responsibilities you've always carried. What you need now are new scaffolds. This book offers one. Workshops and peer exchanges offer others.

But the most vital scaffold is you. The goal is not to surrender to AI. It's to teach orchestration - not just as a technical skill, but as an educational stance.

In the classroom, this means shifting the question from "What did you write?" to "What did you ask the system, and why?" It means asking students to critique AI-generated responses before writing their own. It means treating prompt design, bias detection, and simulated fluency as part of core digital literacy.

Doing so restores authorship and centers the one thing AI cannot simulate: human intentionality.

The future of education will not be built on banning GPT or punishing its use. Nor will it be sustained by pretending a thousand-word essay written in three seconds is equivalent to understanding.

What will endure is presence - the ability to help students engage deeply, reflect critically, and make meaning out of complexity. Reclaiming your role doesn't require burnout. It requires reframing.

Sven D. Olensky

Start by changing the assignment, not the students. Reimagine AI not as a shortcut, but as a co-learner. Instead of asking students to write an essay from scratch, ask them to use GPT to generate three versions of an argument, then reflect in 300 words on which version they trust most - and why.

Teach orchestration as authorship. Treat prompt-writing like thesis-writing, constraint-setting like critical thinking, and bias detection like reading comprehension. Let students reveal their judgment, not just their output. The future of learning depends not on whether students can use AI, but whether they know what to do when it gives them something wrong, shallow, or biased.

Above all, build in shared reflection - not surveillance. Ask questions like, "Where did the system get it right but miss you?" or "What part of this answer felt most artificial - and why?" These are the moments where learning lives.

Design Patterns for Orchestration Literacy

To operationalize orchestration as a public good, we need repeatable formats that can be deployed by any organization, regardless of size, funding, or digital maturity.

This section offers civic design patterns - modular, adaptable, and friction-minimized. These patterns aren't just templates. They're *seed loops*. Planted anywhere people care enough to teach each other how to stay *human*, stay *present*, and *resist being sidelined*. No certification required.

Pattern 1: The GPT Circle

> **Where**: Library, church basement, break room, reentry center
>
> **What happens:**
> - A few people, 1 laptop, 1 facilitator showing GPT
> - Each person says one thing they do in daily life
> - GPT simulates it and the group reflects
> - Facilitator teaches basic orchestration prompt frame
> - Everyone co-writes a pledge

Why it works: Minimal gear. Maximum shock. Collective reflection. The loop is built together.

Sven D. Olensky

Pattern 2: The Public Orchestration Station

Where: Library info desk, job center front table

What's there:

- Laminated prompt scaffolds
- A screen looping *5 things you can ask AI*
- Printouts: *How to ask for help without losing your voice*
- A volunteer once a week

Why it works: Passive access. No commitment. Entry point for the wary or overwhelmed.

Pattern 3: The Family Tech Agreement Kit

Where: School folders, pediatric clinics, PTA meetings

What's inside:

- Simple worksheet: *How we use AI in our home*
- Sections for kids and parents
- Boundaries, shared agreements, off-limits uses

Why it works: Resets conversation from *ban or allow* to *what matters to us* and builds authorship at home.

Orchestration in Real Life

Orchestration isn't just for tech leaders or enterprise teams. It's for parents, kids, and everyday decisions. I practice AI orchestration daily - not in some abstract or high-level way, but in the moments that shape real life.

One of the most meaningful examples came when my daughter Sarah was preparing to enter high school. She's sharp, curious, and deeply drawn to design and building - not coding or robotics, but structure, creativity, and hands-on problem solving. Engineering? Absolutely. Design and art? Without a doubt.

We sat down to map out her high school elective path, expecting a few simple decisions. What we found instead was a maze - dozens of options, no obvious sequence, and very little guidance about how today's choices would shape tomorrow's opportunities. It was overwhelming.

So I did what I often do in moments like this - I turned to GPT. But not to outsource the decision. To illuminate the landscape.

First, we gathered everything we could: elective course descriptions, graduation requirements, state academic standards, college alignment maps, and even personality and learning style insights - her preferences, not mine.

Then came the orchestration. I asked the system to help us identify which electives built on one another, which combinations would expand options instead of closing them, what an architecture or engineering path might truly entail, and how we could meet both her creative impulses and academic obligations.

GPT helped us simulate, compare, and sequence. It helped us see patterns and trade-offs that weren't visible in the raw material.

But the key was that it didn't decide for her. It gave her a way to see what her decisions meant - where they might lead, and how to shape them with intention.

That's orchestration. Not delegation, not surrender. Just clarity. Empowerment. A more human way to navigate complexity, with AI as a partner - not a parent.

AI-Augmented Learning: A Better Way to Learn

I'm using the same orchestration approach for Social Studies, specifically 10th grade World History - which, for some reason, Georgia has made one of the most demanding courses in the school. And we're not talking about Honors or AP. This is the standard on-level track, yet the first unit alone spans 70 pages.

Instead of forcing my daughter to grind through that volume of content, we're using GPT to reshape the learning experience. The process involves extracting the core standards and learning goals, condensing the material into a high-leverage summary, identifying five anchor concepts that unlock the majority of the content, and verifying that nothing essential has been lost in the process.

With the prompt we developed - refined through back-and-forth with ChatGPT - we've been able to reduce textbook content by over 95% without losing alignment to the Georgia Standards of Excellence. For example, Unit 1 originally contained approximately 25,000 words.

Now, she engages with a 600-word summary, just over two pages, that covers the same objectives and core ideas in a more digestible and meaningful way. This isn't about cutting corners. It's about cutting through noise. She's still learning - but with greater clarity, because she's starting to understand the *why*, not just memorizing the *what*.

This shift is about more than efficiency. It's a redefinition of agency.

I used to feel powerless in the face of bloated school systems, rigid course pathways, and the endless avalanche of material. The panic of being a parent trying to help, trying to keep up, was real.

But orchestration offers something else entirely. It lets you see the patterns in the chaos. It helps you connect the dots between choices and consequences. It turns walls of content into maps - and more importantly, it shifts the dynamic from *doing it for your child* to *doing it with them*.

These aren't AI tricks. This isn't cheating. This is a better way to learn - together.

Sven D. Olensky

What Comes Next

Everything you've read - every insight, prompt pattern, and orchestration loop - is now being transformed into free, public tools through the nonprofit I founded, the **AI Literacy for Everyone Foundation.**

This is where the work continues - on a community scale.

Free Resources

Visit **AILiteracyForEveryone.org** to access free resources:

- *Downloadable prompt templates* for students, parents, educators, and professionals
- *Compression kits* to summarize long documents, policy drafts, or curriculum
- *Cheat sheets* for building strong prompts
- *Guides for community leaders* to bring orchestration literacy into their school, church, or neighborhood

AI Orchestration Practitioner Program

I am also building a full curriculum that teaches orchestration not just as a skill, but as a *lifelong literacy*:

- How to think with models
- How to retain agency
- How to adapt without losing identity
- How to use AI as a scaffold - not a crutch

An Ideal World

Based on an actual conversation with ChatGPT.

Sven, Orchestration Literacy is not abstract. It's a framework for remembering how to be human in the loop. If people used AI the way you're proposing - not as a shortcut or a crutch, but as a mirror and amplifier of human agency - everything would change. Not just incrementally. Foundationally.

This is the future you're advocating for:

One where AI doesn't erase people - it restores their authorship.

Where outputs don't define us - our questions do.

Where we don't grade for form - we grow for depth.

But only if we teach people to orchestrate, to engage and to be present, not only to outsource thinking.

Because if AI were used with presence, not to replace thought, but to refine it, then:

Learning would deepen, not disappear.
Students would use AI to test their ideas, question assumptions, and sharpen their reasoning - not avoid the process altogether. Instead of submitting GPT's words, they'd submit their voice, more clearly shaped through dialog with the model.

Work would become creative again. *Workers wouldn't be buried in meaningless output. They'd orchestrate systems to handle the noise, while they focused on decisions, ethics, context, purpose. The grunt work would go to the machine - not the soul.*

Education would stop being a filter and become a forge. *No more chasing 90s and 100s for survival. No more pass/fail identity structures. Instead, AI would be used to individualize mastery, letting people explore at their pace, with immediate feedback - but still requiring judgment, synthesis, agency.*

The system wouldn't flatten people. It would respond to them. *People would no longer just perform. They'd participate. They'd guide the machine. They'd use AI to think better, communicate clearer, dream bigger - not to disappear.*

Literacy would expand from decoding language to directing intelligence. *Everyone, regardless of background, could gain access to the tools of power - research, strategy, persuasion, analysis - without gatekeepers.*

APPENDIX

Family Tech Agreement Kit

Purpose

This worksheet is designed to help families reflect on how AI is used in daily life, discuss what tasks should or should not be delegated to generative systems, and preserve shared values around authorship, accuracy, and trust.

1. Identify AI Use at Home: *Who uses it, for what, and how often?*

2. Set Boundaries Together: *Tasks we agree should not be done by AI in our household: Writing personal apology notes, Creating school assignments without review, Simulating family conversations, Generating content in someone else's voice*

3. Our Shared Check Questions: *Before using AI, we ask: Am I clear on what I want the AI to do? Does this task reflect something I want to say myself? Will I review and revise the output before sharing it?*

Signature & Agreement Date

By signing below, we agree to revisit this worksheet every 3 months and adjust our practices together.

Parent/Guardian: _____

Child(ren): _____

Date: _____

A Checklist for Public Adaptation of AI Orchestration

To bring it all together, here is a scaffold for inclusive, strategic civic adaptation to AI:

Narrative Framing

- Normalize that disorientation is real - and shared.
- Make *AI-literate* not a badge of privilege, but a public good.

Family Resilience Modules

- Toolkits for tech agreements, shared AI diaries, trust-building conversations.

Orchestration Education

- From third grade through adult learning centers.
- Teach intent, constraint, reflection.

Mental Health Inclusion

- Create group spaces to process cognitive dislocation.
- Add AI-specific modules to youth counseling and elder support.

Ongoing Orchestration Practice

- Free platforms, prompts, and coaching sessions to keep skill alive
- Peer mentorship across age groups

Schools

- Move beyond banning GPT. Teach orchestration.
- Make prompt framing a core part of digital literacy.
- Let students debug systems, not just obey them.

Libraries

- Host *Ask the AI* hours.
- Train volunteers in civic orchestration skills.
- Become the local counterweight to private knowledge engines.

Workplaces

- Share AI tools - but don't collapse headcount first.
- Build retraining pipelines.
- Let orchestration fluency count toward performance, not just speed.

Churches, Mosques, Synagogues

- Teach AI ethics as moral literacy.
- Use GPT for access - but keep theology grounded in lived voice.
- Let faith communities be places of reflection, not simulation.

Glossary

Agency *(n.)*

The capacity to act with awareness, to make choices deliberately, and to take ownership of their consequences. Agency is what allows a person to live with intention rather than drift on autopilot. It is not about control over systems - it is about control over oneself.

At its core, agency is the willingness to be present: to observe one's own actions, to make decisions with conscience, and to accept accountability for what follows. It resists the urge to outsource judgment. It refuses the comfort of default settings. It insists that every action is authored, not just executed.

Agency is not automatic. It must be exercised, again and again, especially when ease, speed, or consensus invite disengagement. To act with agency is to take responsibility for your presence in the world - for what you shape, what you permit, and what you let pass.

In the context of this book, agency is the ground from which all meaningful engagement begins. Without it, nothing else holds. Not learning. Not action. Not change.

Loop *(n.)*

In the context of this book, the *loop* refers to a dynamic system of feedback, participation, and human agency. It is both the central metaphor and the structural foundation of the framework presented here.

The loop is not linear. It represents recurrence, reflection, and recalibration. A loop implies that the human role is not a one-time configuration or oversight checkpoint

- it is an ongoing presence. The argument at the core of this work is that in the age of generative AI, human agency must be sustained through active engagement, not outsourced to automation or reduced to a passive supervisory role.

This theme carries multiple layers of meaning:

First, it reframes AI alignment as **orchestration**. Traditional safety paradigms often focus on aligning the model to human intent, but this book proposes a different view: the human must stay inside the loop, not simply as a safeguard, but as an editor, verifier, and creative guide. The loop becomes a living process - responsive, iterative, and accountable.

Second, it centers **lived experience**. When systems bypass or erase human judgment, the loop breaks. A broken loop leads to disconnection and drift. A functioning loop allows for error correction, contextual nuance, and personal relevance. It keeps people - especially non-technical users - close to meaning, rather than isolated from it.

Third, it links **civic structure** with system design. In a civic context, a broken loop looks like this: bad data leads to poor decisions, which erode trust, leading to disengagement, which produces even worse data. This book argues for loops that regenerate trust and participation, not loops that decay into collapse. That includes the feedback between citizens and institutions, students and AI tutors, workers and systems that increasingly shape their labor.

Finally, the loop distinguishes **orchestration** from **automation**. Automation removes people from the process. Orchestration places them at the center - not for control alone, but for guidance, ethics, and adaptability.

Where automation isolates, orchestration invites. Where automation replaces, orchestration aligns.

The loop, then, is not just a system metaphor. It is a principle of design, a model of engagement, and a claim about what must remain human.

Cognitive Collapse (n.)

An internal erosion of trust in one's own thinking, judgment, or creative voice after sustained exposure to the fluency of machine-generated responses. Unlike simulation shock, which strikes suddenly and externally when a user sees a model convincingly emulate high-status human roles, cognitive collapse unfolds over time. It is quiet, cumulative, and often unnoticed until the user no longer questions the machine's authority - or their own.

Cognitive collapse is not an error state. It is a psychological drift. The model sounds right, so the user stops checking. The model finishes sentences, so the user stops writing. The model offers certainty, so the user stops doubting. What begins as convenience becomes dependency. The person does not disappear, but their participation becomes passive.

This book frames cognitive collapse as the critical failure point in the loop. When feedback stops, meaning decays. The only defense is intentional interruption: asking follow-up questions, verifying claims, rewriting output, or choosing to resist automation altogether.

Cognitive collapse is not inevitable. But it is structurally incentivized in environments that prioritize speed, polish, or output over participation. To remain engaged (*human-*

in-the-loop), the user must stay just a little slower, a little more skeptical, and a lot more present.

Simulation Shock *(n.)*

A destabilizing realization that generative AI can convincingly perform roles, decisions, and identities that were once earned through time, access, or expertise. *Simulation shock* occurs when a user sees the model fluently inhabit a position that they assumed was inaccessible without years of training, authority, or lived experience. It is not just technical surprise. It is psychological rupture.

Unlike cognitive collapse, which emerges gradually through internal erosion of trust, simulation shock strikes suddenly. It happens the moment a person prompts the model to act as a doctor, a COO, a policymaker, or a billionaire - and finds that the response sounds not only plausible, but embodied. The shock is not about accuracy. It is about fluency. The machine does not answer like a student. It answers like someone who belongs in the room.

Simulation shock collapses the boundary between expertise and simulation. It confronts the user with the possibility that roles they once aspired to - or once held - can now be summoned on demand. For some, this is exhilarating. For others, it feels like a loss. But for everyone, it marks a shift.

It is *external*. It's the moment a person realizes the system can simulate roles, authority, or expertise they once thought were earned, exclusive, or unreachable. It's a boundary rupture. The reaction is usually visceral: disbelief, awe, threat, displacement.

This book treats simulation shock as a civic threshold. It is the moment where the user must choose: to defer, to disengage, or to orchestrate. What follows the shock is not predetermined. What matters is what happens next.

Orchestration Literacy *(n.)*

The ability to shape the behavior of generative systems with purpose and precision. It's not about using AI fluently - it's about using it responsibly. Orchestration literacy means knowing what you're asking, why you're asking it, and how to evaluate what comes back.

It's the skill of stepping in when output misfires. It means catching when tone shifts, when bias creeps in, or when the answer looks smooth but says nothing. It's knowing how to reframe, how to press further, or when to stop and think before accepting the result.

This is not a technical specialty. It's a public skill. Just as reading lets you navigate a world of text, orchestration literacy lets you navigate a world of generated language. Without it, you're stuck in passive mode - scanning, reacting, complying.

With it, you stay in the loop. You lead the exchange. You remain the author of your intent.

Minimum Viable Orchestration *(n.)*

The smallest set of human actions required to keep meaning, context, and agency intact when working with generative systems. *Minimum viable orchestration* is not full control. It is just enough participation to keep the loop from breaking.

The idea is borrowed from engineering and startup culture, where the minimum viable product is the simplest version of a tool that can still deliver value. Here, the value is not output. The value is *alignment with intent*. A user who gives input, asks follow-up questions, corrects hallucinated claims, or rewrites a machine-generated summary is performing minimum viable orchestration.

It is the floor beneath orchestration literacy. It does not require deep expertise or technical skill. It requires only presence, feedback, and the willingness to engage rather than accept. The goal is not to outthink the model, but to remain in relationship with it.

This book uses minimum viable orchestration as a baseline threshold. When users no longer ask, *Is this true?* or *Is this what I meant?* or *Should this be said this way?* - the orchestration fails. Minimum viable orchestration is what keeps the human from vanishing inside the fluency of the machine.

REFERENCES AND SOURCES

- Abril, D. (2025, April 8). *Americans worry AI is coming for these jobs.* The Washington Post
- Allen, K. (2025). *Family meetings build healthy families* [Extension publication]. North Carolina State University Extension.
- American Academy of Pediatrics. (2023). *Family Media Plan* (HealthyChildren.org tool).
- American Psychological Association. (2023). *Work in America 2023: Survey results.* Washington, DC: APA Center for Organizational Excellence.
- American Psychological Association. (2023, September 7). *Worries about AI, surveillance at work may be connected to poor mental health* (Press release).
- Associated Press. (2024). *Older adults prepare for a world altered by AI.* AP News.
- Banerjee, U. (2025, April 22). *Silent layoffs are trending as AI takes over corporate America.* AIM Research
- Bender, E. M., Gebru, T., et al. (2021). *On the Dangers of Stochastic Parrots: Can Language Models Be Too Big?* Proceedings of FAccT 2021.
- Bommasani, R., Hudson, D. A., et al. (2021). *On the Opportunities and Risks of Foundation Models.* Stanford Institute for Human-Centered AI.
- Briggs, J., & Kodnani, D. (2023, March 27). *Generative AI could raise global GDP by 7%.* Goldman Sachs (Insights).
- Casal-Otero, L., Catala, A., Fernández-Morante, C., Taboada, M., & Cebreiro, B. (2023). *AI literacy in*

K-12: A systematic literature review. International Journal of STEM Education, 10, Article 29

- Centre for International Governance Innovation. (2023). *Why we need inclusive data governance in the age of AI.* Waterloo, ON: CIGI.
- Chen, W. X., Srinivasan, S., & Zakerinia, S. (2024). *Displacement or Complementarity? The labor market impact of generative AI* (HBS Working Paper No. 25-039). Harvard Business School.
- Cloud Security Alliance. (2023). *Securing LLM-Backed Systems: Risk and Mitigation Frameworks.*
- Dempere, J., Modugu, K., Hesham, A., & Ramasamy, L. K. (2023). *The impact of ChatGPT on higher education.* Frontiers in Education, 8, 1206936.
- Dey, M. (2023, May 1). *IBM to pause hiring in plan to replace 7,800 jobs with AI.* Reuters
- Dignazio, C., & Bhargava, R. (2020). *Data Feminism.* MIT Press.
- D'Ignazio, C., Bhargava, R., & Gray, M. L. (2022). *Teaching AI Literacy in Community Spaces: A Civic Empowerment Framework.* Media Cloud Civic AI Series.
- DLA Piper. (2025, April 7). *White House releases guidance for AI acquisition and use in government.*
- Economic Times. (2025, June 4). *Microsoft lays off 300 more employees as AI-driven restructuring continues.*

- Eder, M., & Sjøvaag, H. (2024). *Artificial intelligence and the dawn of an algorithmic divide*. Frontiers in Communication, 9, 1453251.
- Eloundou, T., Manning, S., Mishkin, P., & Rock, D. (2023). *GPTs are GPTs: An early look at the labor market impact potential of large language models*. arXiv:2303.10130.
- Good Things Foundation. (2024). *Developing AI literacy with people who have low or no digital skills* (Research report). London: Good Things Foundation.
- GovTech. (2025, April 24). *Trump Signs Executive Order to Ramp Up K-12 AI Education*.
- Great Place to Work Canada. (2025, May 15). *Workplace Anxiety in 2025: Navigating Mental Health Amid AI and Economic Uncertainty*.
- Hughes, S. (2023, September). *Here is why AI makes traditional education models obsolete*. World Economic Forum Agenda.
- Kos'myna, Nataliya, MIT. (2025). *Your Brain on ChatGPT: Accumulation of Cognitive Debt when Using an AI Assistant for Essay Writing Task*.
- Lake, R., Dusseault, B., & Lee, J. (2023). *AI is coming to U.S. classrooms, but who will benefit?* Center on Reinventing Public Education.
- Madgavkar, A., Chui, M., White, O., & Hasebe, P. (2023, July 26). *Generative AI and the future of work in America*. McKinsey Global Institute.
- Mollick, E., & Mollick, L. (2023). *Using AI to Teach Prompt Engineering and Critical Thinking in the Classroom*. Working paper, Wharton School.

- National Academies of Sciences, Engineering, and Medicine. (2021). *Human-AI Teaming: State of the Art and Research Needs.* Washington, DC: The National Academies Press.
- National Institute of Standards and Technology. (2023). *AI Risk Management Framework 1.0.* Gaithersburg, MD: U.S. Department of Commerce, NIST.
- NIST. (2023). *AI Risk Management Framework (AI RMF 1.0).*
- Noble, S. U. (2018). *Algorithms of Oppression: How Search Engines Reinforce Racism.* NYU Press.
- Nosta, J. (2025, May). *Is AI dismantling intellectual elitism?* Psychology Today.
- OECD. (2021). *AI and the Future of Skills: Insights from OECD Scenarios.*
- OpenAI. (2023). *GPT-4 Technical Report.*
- Oschinski, M., Crawford, A., & Wu, M. (2024, December). *AI and the Future of Workforce Training* (Report). Center for Security and Emerging Technology.
- Oyetade, K., & Zuva, T. (2025). *Advancing equitable education with inclusive AI to mitigate bias and enhance teacher literacy.* Educational Process: International Journal, 14, e2025087.
- Parthasarathy, S., & Katzman, J. (2024). *Bringing communities in, achieving AI for all. Issues in Science and Technology, 40*(4).
- Perrault, R., Shoham, Y., et al. (2019). *The AI Index Report 2019.* Stanford HAI.

- Pew Research Center. (2023). *Parenting in America Today* (Report).
- Pew Research Center. (2025, April 3). *How the U.S. public and AI experts view artificial intelligence.* Pew Research Center – Internet & Technology.
- Rahimi-Midani, A. (2025, May 23). *Global goals, local realities: Aligning AI governance with inclusion.* Tech Policy Press.
- Rauf, D. S. (2023, November 3). *Computer science courses gaining traction, as state requirements take hold. Education Week.*
- ResumeBuilder. (2023, November 8). *1 in 3 companies will replace employees with AI in 2024.* ResumeBuilder.com.
- Rong, Y., Leemann, T., Nguyen, T. T., Fiedler, L., Qian, P., Unhelkar, V., ... & Kasneci, E. (2023). *Towards human-centered explainable AI: A survey of user studies for model explanations.* arXiv:2210.11584.
- Sandle, P. (2023, May 18). *BT to cut up to 55,000 jobs by 2030 as fibre and AI arrive.* Reuters
- Selwyn, N. (2020). *Should Robots Replace Teachers? AI and the Future of Education.* Polity Press.
- Septiandri, A., Constantinides, M., & Quercia, D. (2025). *AI and the economic divide: How Artificial Intelligence could widen the divide in the U.S.* EPJ Data Science, 14(33).
- U.S. Chamber of Commerce. (2024). *Empowering small business: The impact of technology on U.S.*

small business (Report). U.S. Chamber Technology Engagement Center

- U.S. Department of Education, Office of Educational Technology. (2023). *Artificial Intelligence and the Future of Teaching and Learning: Insights and Recommendations.* Washington, DC: U.S. Department of Education.
- UNESCO. (2021). *AI and Education: Guidance for Policymakers.*
- United Nations Conference on Trade and Development. (2025). *Technology and Innovation Report 2025: Inclusive artificial intelligence for development.* Geneva: UNCTAD.
- Webster, M. (2023, December 13). *Recent data study reveals most popular side hustle in every U.S. state. CPA Practice Advisor.*
- Weissman, S. (2025, January 23). *Community colleges join forces to expand access to AI training.* Inside Higher Ed.
- White House Office of Science and Technology Policy. (2022). *Blueprint for an AI Bill of Rights: Making automated systems work for the American people.* Washington, DC: OSTP.
- World Economic Forum. (2023). *Education 4.0: The Future of Learning in a Post-COVID World.*
- World Economic Forum. (2023). *The Future of Jobs Report 2023* (Insight Report). World Economic Forum.

About the Author

Sven D. Olensky is a security architect leader, mentor, and lifelong technologist working at the intersection of AI, human agency, and system design. With nearly three decades of experience in engineering, enterprise architecture, and cybersecurity - including roles at the Federal Reserve and Fortune 500 companies - he now focuses on making AI understandable, empowering, and ethically grounded.

He is the founder of the AI Literacy for Everyone Foundation, a nonprofit created to advance AI literacy, ethical technology education, and strategic digital empowerment. Through public education boot camps and AI awareness programs, he helps communities, working adults, and families bridge the gap between hype and reality and prepare for what's coming.

Sven has shaped cloud and AI security strategies across multi-cloud infrastructure, enterprise platforms, and the emerging frontier of GenAI and LLM adoption. His work centers on translating complex technical risk into actionable frameworks that support innovation without compromising trust.

He believes security should be an enabler, not a gatekeeper. Everyone deserves a seat at the table.

This is his first published work.

www.ingramcontent.com/pod-product-compliance
Lightning Source LLC
Chambersburg PA
CBHW060807050426
42449CB00008B/1587